Fairy Gardens

A Guide to Growing an
Enchanted Miniature World

Betty Earl

B. B. Mackey Books, Wayne, Pennsylvania

FAIRY GARDENS
A Guide to Growing
an Enchanted Miniature World

Betty Earl

First Edition, April, 2012
B. B. Mackey Books, Publisher
P. O. Box 475
Wayne, PA 19087
www.mackeybooks.com

Copyright © 2012 by Betty Earl, Author

Photographers:
Betty Earl, author and main photographer
Jeremie Corp.
Landscapes in Miniature
Miniature Garden Shoppe
Wholesale Fairy Gardens
Nancy Bowley/Longwood Gardens
Google, Inc (Ann Arbor office)
Iseli Nursery
Kappi Veenendaal (Holland)
Duane Campbell
Bob Foran Photography
Urban Fairies Operations (Ann Arbor)
Betty Mackey

Front Cover photo by Betty Earl
Back Cover photos, counter clockwise from top, Nancy Bowley, Betty Earl, Jeremie Corp., Miniature Garden Shoppe, Landscapes in Miniature
Title page photo by Miniature Garden Shoppe
Paperback Garden

ISBN 978-1-893443-50-1

Library of Congress Cataloging in Publication Data
Earl, Betty, 1943-

CIP data pending

Chapter 1: What is a Fairy Garden? ...... P. 7

Chapter 2: What or Who are the Fairies? ...... P. 11

Chapter 3: Creating a Successful Fairy Garden ...... P. 17
Children and Fairy Gardens ...... P. 18
Your Own Fairy Garden ...... P. 21
Locating Your Outdoor Fairy Garden ...... P. 23
Pick a Theme ...... P. 25
Fairy Houses ...... P. 26
Fairy Doors ...... P. 29

Chapter 4: Combining and Adding Plants and Accessories ...... P. 33
Plants for Outdoor Fairy Gardens ...... P. 36
Indoor (Dish) Container Fairy Gardens ...... P. 44
Fairy Garden Accessories ...... P. 48
Adding Fairies ...... P. 50

Chapter 5: Gardening with the Fairies ...... P. 51
A Sampling of Fairy Legends ...... P. 52
Flowers and Plants for Fairy Use ...... P. 53
Flowers and Plants Associated with Fairies ...... P. 55
Cicely Mary Barker's Flower Fairies ...... P. 61

Chapter 6: Planting and Maintenance of Fairy Gardens ...... P. 63

Further Reading, Resources, and Index ...... P. 72

Jeremie Corp.

Betty Mackey

3

Set atop a light-colored flat stone patio, the dark rustic wire bistro set is the perfect spot for fairies to rest at the end of a long day. Photo courtesy of Miniature Garden Shoppe.

FOREWORD

As a young child, I firmly believed in fairies, and that these sprites, though invisible, were everywhere. Belief and supposition were enough. I never ever gave any serious thought to where fairies might live.

So imagine my amazement when as a mature adult, I learned so much about the subject of fairies, which at the time seemed to be merely a childhood fascination. This led me to the realization, whether we admit it or not, that there remains a little of that innocent child in all of us.

As a bona-fide plantaholic, I am always up for a garden visit. Rain, storms, heat…it doesn't matter. If there's a garden walk, I'm there. For gardening is one of those delicious activities that, once it gets in your blood, you are never sated. There's always one more garden to visit, one more plant to discover, one more perennial to drool over, one more "found" idea to add to your own garden.

Thus it was with fairy gardens. From the very first simple fairy garden in a container by the front door to that elaborate, almost majestic fairy abode in a woodland setting which I saw this past summer, it's been a magical ride. I've met gardeners who truly believe in fairies, fondly recalling childhood experiences of connecting with them, and I've met folks who scoff at the idea that fairies are real, yet are inspired by the merriment of a fairy garden and the illusion of fairies living there.

What I have learned from these gardeners is that there's an enthralling fairy realm out there just waiting to be discovered. Whether you share this adventure with your kids, your friends, your par-

ents, or by yourself, creating a fairy garden allows all to develop a sense of wonder, creativity, and appreciation of nature while at the same time, inspiring one of the most delightful, fairy-filled experiences possible. This is a quest to be cherished forever, for it reminds us of the importance of play.

After all, gardening, though work at times, is pure fun! Or it should be. And nothing brings a smile to your face as quickly as the sight of a fairy door at a base of a tree, a fairy figurine peeking around a fern frond—or if you are truly lucky—the sight of fairies dancing.

Betty Earl

5

THANK YOU

"Hand in hand, with fairy grace, Will we sing, and bless this place"
~~~~ William Shakespeare

Betty Earl

So many people contributed to my understanding of fairy gardens and to the making of this book. Among them is my friend, Deb Wiley, who for many years has shared her time, knowledge and insight whenever I appealed to her kind graces. I am also grateful to Diana Stoll, Joannie Rocchi and Kyle Lambert, for their contagious enthusiasm for the "wee folk," as well as the gracious homeowners who invited me into their yards to view and photograph their whimsical creations.

For some lively conversations and their generous contribution of charming photographs I wish to express my gratitude to Sandy Dittmar, Linda Geho, Courtney Guy, Kelley Howard, Patti Kuhlman, Cathryn Low, Kathryn Newman, Pam Shank, Nancy Bowley, Kappi Veenendaal, Duane Campbell, and Jonathan Wright—you were vital to the richness of this book. To Neil Gaiman and Charles de Lint, your delicious verse on fairies is a work of art in itself and I appreciate the privilege of sharing these pieces with my readers.

Many thanks to my publisher, Betty Mackey, for her belief that the time had come for this book, for her elegant design, and for pulling it all together with such thoughtfulness and artistry. And finally, to my husband, David, a very special thank you for reading the text—not that easy a task for a non-gardening engineer—and for putting up with my long absences while I shut myself in the office in order to finish this "tome."

~~~~Betty Earl

CHAPTER 1: WHAT IS A FAIRY GARDEN?

"And as the seasons come and go, here's something you might like to know. There are fairies everywhere: under bushes, in the air, playing games just like you play, singing through their busy day. So listen, touch, and look around – in the air and on the ground. And if you watch all nature's things, you might just see a fairy's wing."

~~~~ Author Unknown

Betty Earl

For centuries mankind has been fascinated by legends of fairies, the "wee folk" who can be kind to us humans or be mean and mischievous. While concrete evidence of the existence of fairies is, naturally, rather hard to come by, adding fairy gardens within our landscapes is one charming way we can participate in this centuries-old tradition. This encourages people of all ages to flex their mental wings and imagine the existence of fairies. With a bit of fairy lore, some imagination, and just a small patch of space you can create a garden of whimsy, an open invitation to fairies to come and frolic. Whether fairies arrive or not, your inner child will soar.

Fairy gardens are miniature gardens within the landscape that, with their small plants, houses, outdoor structures, and furnishing, give the illusion of tiny creatures living there. Fairy gardens can be any size or shape from the very small, constructed completely within containers displayed on tabletops, to larger, grander scenes at the base of a tree, under a shrub, tucked inside an old birdbath, or peeking out from under a prized hosta leaf.

By artfully placing a door at the base of a tree trunk to indicate the entry to a home inside, a dollhouse-sized bench on a field of moss, or a birdbath the size of your little finger next to a border of mini-roses, you are making a fairy garden that adds an element of surprise and playfulness to the yard.

Who or what are the fairies? (in Chapter 2). While children need no excuse to believe in fairies, this belief is not universally accepted among adults. The fairy gardens of believers are meant to attract fairies from their otherworldly realm in hopes of persuading them to take up permanent residence in ours. For non-believers, the objective is to create a sense of magic, nostalgia, and fun and share it with visitors of any age.

William Shakespeare described fairies as diminutive, sometimes trouble-some creatures. Victorian era painters bewitched the populace with works of art depicting garden fairies as the cause of all sort of mischief while running chaotically among their bigger human counterparts. Legends tell of mischievous supernatural creatures with either wicked or good moral traits, depending on the situation or their mood. When something came up missing, it was said to be the fault of the bad imp; when a gift appeared unexpectedly, it was the work of a good fairy.

All of this may have been inspired by the fairy folklore of the Middle Ages where many tales of fairies— usually Irish or Welsh—were considered to be truthful accounts as if these fairies danced and played every day in the surrounding forests, fields, and hillsides.

The people at Disney helped to change our views of fairies, for their talented graphic artists and popular movies, *Fantasia* and *Peter Pan*, presented fairies as the tiny yet beautiful and benevolent gossamer-winged creatures we think of today.

Thinking about design (in Chapters 3 and 4). When designing a

fairy garden, consider how you want to portray the world of fairies. Through accessories and plants, you can show the lighter, fairy-princess fantasy of little girls everywhere, or, as in ancient times, reveal a darker, more somber side of the wee folk.

Ideally, fairy gardens are located in small, somewhat secluded parts of the garden, giving the visitor the feeling that they just happened to stumble upon a magical place. They can be planted in the garden, on a tree stump, beneath a bush, or upon a whole special section of the garden. When we place a door, a house, or a pond in this special garden, we are sending a message that this is a "fairy friendly" garden—a safe haven to which we welcome them.

As with any project, knowledge of the subject matter is important for success. You do not need to believe in these mythical creatures to create a fairy garden, but it is wise to learn what fairies are supposed to prefer in their environment if you want to entice them to your yard.

If you are not sure where to begin, start small. Create a container fairy garden. This allows even apartment and condo dwellers lacking a back yard to have one. Any pot or container will do, but shallow bowls or troughs with drainage holes and large open surface areas work best.

Use plants with miniature leaves and low stature, dwarf plants that naturally stay small or can easily be pruned and shaped to resemble larger plants such as shrubs or trees. Plants that are generally used for bonsai work well, as do miniature rock garden shrubs and herbs such as small-leafed basil, rosemary and creeping thyme.

Visit garden centers and nurseries that sell succulents, cacti, moss, and miniature strains of flowering plants, such as African violets, cape primrose (*Streptocarpus*), cyclamen and dwarf fuchsia. Miniature structures such as arbors and pathways help to define the space and give your fairy garden a personal touch. Add tiny furniture and sparkly ornaments or crystals to tempt the fairies, and you have the beginnings of a garden that will mesmerize your winged guests.

The plantings in an indoor fairy garden need light, like other houseplants, so place the container near a window but out of the reach of hot afternoon sun.

In the garden you'll need a modest, sheltered area because small plants and delicate miniature accessories require protection from the elements,

Betty Earl

rowdy garden visitors, and rambling feet. Take advantage of your natural landscape and create your fairy garden in the shade of a tree, under a bush, or nestled against a stump or rock. Now would be a good time to decide the size and shape of your fairy garden. Although gardens are always evolving, having a good idea of what you want this garden to be will keep you from adding so many things as to look chaotic.

It's wise to plan your garden before you go and buy plants. Do you want a mostly green garden, one rich with blossoms, surrounded by sweet scented herbs, or a captivating mixture of all of the above? Study flower catalogs to determine which plants might be best suited for your garden. Visit your local nursery, look around, and ask for their help.

Gardening with the fairies (Chapter 5). There are certain flowers, herbs, and plants that have long been associated with fairies, but if those plants don't fit your garden, don't fret. Instead, select plants that are suited to your garden theme and growing conditions, be it sun or shade, making sure they are small enough to be in scale with a fairy garden.

Fairies are said to be partial to the hiding places of the garden, such as a miniature fern grove in a secluded corner of the yard, the hollow of a rotten log, or a clearing at the base of a tree. They favor gardens with wildflowers and a slightly unkept look, as well as thyme and moss for the soft meadow needed for sleeping, dancing, and playing.

Since fairies need space for celebrations and merry-making, lay down small stones and pebbles for pathways and patios. Tiny benches, chairs, fencing, and arbors not only add to the large garden feel, but also encourage fairies to stay. And of course, no fairy garden is complete without a scattering of fairy dust, which looks like opalescent glitter. You can add a fairy figure or leave it as it is for the fairies to find.

If you live near a small stream, you may have water fairies in your garden. Fairies are thought to love the sounds, sights, and feel of water. If your landscape doesn't have a stream, a tiny pond will suit them just as well.

Weatherproof dollhouse-style furniture, miniature glazed ornaments, and a small water dish embedded into the garden to resemble a pond can be enticing.

A whimsical fairy door at the base of a tree allows fairies to travel easily between their realm and ours, and to leave quickly should they feel threatened.

If your garden doesn't come together all at once, don't fret. Part of the fun and pleasure of making a fairy garden is finding just the right pieces to create your perfect garden.

There are no set rules or rigid instructions. These are gardens of whimsy, limited only by your bountiful imagination. Think of acorn caps as fairy cups, walnut shells as fairy bowls, and small champagne glasses as birdbaths.

Fairy gardens are an engaging hobby to practice with your kids, grandkids, friends, or by yourself. Tap into the minds of your children for ideas. Building a fairy garden together is a way to share the fun, wonder and magic of gardening.

Signs of fairy presence. Folklore tells us how to verify that your miniature garden has enticed the fae to take up residence:

- Plants in the garden thrive and grow more lush and beautiful with each passing day.
- Rings of mushrooms called fairy rings have appeared in your lawn.
- Faint sounds of music with no discernable source are heard.
- There is a peaceful, soothing energy within the garden.
- Lingering traces of fairy dust are seen early in the morning.
- Butterflies, insects, and birds associated with the fairies now dwell within your landscape.

Garden care and planting (Chapter 6). Fairy devotees note that fairies care about the environment, so it might be wise to have a nice clean yard, devoid of litter. However, in her book, *Fairies 101*, Doreen Virtue says that fairies do not like perfectly manicured lawns and gardens, either. Pesticides

offend and repel them, and they will not enter a garden that uses them.

Today's garden fairies are members of a mostly compassionate family of nature spirits, untamed and free, lovingly tending to flowers and trees, dancing, partying and playing with the birds and insects, and valiantly trying to preserve a bit of the wild in the encroaching urban sprawl.

Betty Earl

Betty Mackey

Top, handmade fairy doors leaning up against crumbling tree roots suggest fairies live within. Below, is this a fairy?

9

Betty Earl

A white gazebo at the base of a stairway provides fairies with a shady retreat from the hot afternoon sun, and leads to two wrought iron chairs in an ideal spot to spend the evening with a cup of tea while relaxing with friends.

Chapter 2: Who or What are the Fairies?

"Of all the minor creatures of mythology, fairies are the most beautiful, the most numerous, the most memorable." ~~~~ Andrew Lang

Betty Mackey

Fairies are so prevalent in mythical culture that it is natural to wonder where they came from. In folklore we see that fairies have been with us for ages, their presence acknowledged in ballads, poems and stories. Anecdotes appear in nearly every culture and on most continents. Like vampires, dragons, and other legendary beings, they appear to migrate from the folklore of one culture to the next. It has been assumed that belief in fairies by adults was a dead tradition, yet many people confess that they still believe. And this belief —or enchantment, if you will—has become a cultural obsession with fairies and their gardens.

What or who are the fairies? Most of us think of them as tiny, mystical beings with impish personalities, dressed in flowing, pastel clothing and flitting about on gossamer, butterfly-like wings. Descriptions in stories range from perky little pixie-like creatures that fly magically and do nothing worse than play a few innocent tricks on unsuspecting mortals, to the mysterious and powerful dark forces that possess magic both powerful and frightening. They are thought to have the ability to deceive, bewilder or confuse, or to aid, comfort, and help, all on a whim. Fairy folklore has been found worldwide, and it fills the need to explain the unexplainable.

In folklore there are hundreds of different kinds of fairies. Some of the most common types are tall, angelic beings and short, wizened trolls. Some are tiny creatures, others grotesque; some can fly, others can't; but the one thing they all have in common is that they all can appear and disappear at will. Some tales tell of shape-shifting beings who can change their form.

Many explanations have been given for a belief in fairies. Some say that they are spirits of the dead, or were fallen angels neither bad enough for Hell nor good enough for Heaven. Others thought they were a diminutive race of magical people who were forced into hiding when humans dominated the land. Common Celtic belief is that fairies were driven away by humans to live in the otherworldly realm, but a few have chosen to stay and live among us.

At times fairies were considered to be remnants of pagan faiths and a source of evil. At other times, they were considered to be good and gentle secret helpers to deserving individuals.

Some legends note that fairies had many powers: they could affect the seasons, could turn a good harvest into dust, and could withhold spring

rains, cause drought, and even prolong the winter, causing starvation when food ran out. Puritans classified all fairies as devils, claiming that they were creatures of the purest evil.

Crossing the pond, the belief in these mystical creatures spread to America during the colonization period and is still strong in the Appalachians, Ozarks, and other remote mountainous regions of the USA.

From charming bedtime fairy tales to cautionary narratives of epic bloodshed and misery, fairies have been a favorite topic of conversation for those who love both the fanciful and the perilous.

As can be expected, different societies have come up with various explanations of the origins of these ethereal beings that are at odds with one another. Yet some details are too similar to be dismissed.

Fairies are associated with flowers preferred by bees and butterflies.

Fairies can be lighthearted. Photo courtesy of Longwood Gardens.

It is often said that fairies are tiny, supernatural creatures. For the most part, they are extremely long-lived beings known to possess intimidating magical powers such as the ability to fly, become invisible, and cast imposing spells. Generally humanoid in form, they possess inexplicable attributes, not the least of which are otherworldly beauty and grace, celestial brightness, and wings.

Stories depict fairies in contradictory ways: haughty and meek, indifferent and compassionate, capricious and steadfast, loving and aloof, temperamental, and easy-going. They are often playful and are extraordinarily mischievous. Of course, since fairies are a mystical and ostensibly fictional presence, they are very difficult to categorize.

They are thought to be pagan in origin. Known in some legends as pagan gods and goddesses, the tradition of worshipping these fairy folk quick-ly spread from all branches of the Celtic families to Germany, France, and the British Isles. The Welsh, a matriarchal society, called the fairies The Mothers and often depicted them as women.

Even today, fairy folklore is very much alive in Ireland, where locals say fairies live in the pagan burial mounds scattered about the Irish countryside, and have the ability to freely move in and about the dimensions of earth, the heavens and the underworld. And it is still thought that fairies come out of these, their fairy hills, on Halloween eve.

Those old tales tell of fairies causing disease, plague and even death. They tell of fairies deliberately and maliciously causing harm to innocent people for no discernible reason other than their amusement. And while not all fairies were considered evil, at best they were said to be noncommittal, and except on some very rare occasions, generally not caring a whit about the welfare of mortals. And the idea that fairies can be called upon for help—a belief now prevalent—would have come as a great surprise to many people.

When belief in fairies was common most people didn't mention them by name, referring to them solely as the Little People or the Hidden People. Mortals were to speak well of fairies and treat them with respect, or their anger would be

Betty Earl

Nestled amid rocks and greenery, a fairy grist mill churns out endless natural products for the party loving fairies.

roused. It is traditional to leave small trinkets, such as small sparkly beads, as gifts for fairies to gain their favor.

Folklore tells us that fairies practiced kidnapping. Young and lovely children were supposedly the special objects of desire, and often, when they were snatched away from their homes, ugly, sickly, or frail fairy babies, called changelings, were left in their place. Rituals surrounding futile attempts to "rescue" their stolen children from the fairies included changelings being thrown into water, beaten severely with a switch, left unfed and crying in an open field, or placed on a hot stove. Historians have suggested that the changeling legends were a way for people to cope with and explain away things like birth defects and debilitating infant diseases.

THOUGHTS ON FAIRIES TODAY

It seems that these legends and myths stem from a lack of understanding. Somewhere I once read, "What you do not understand, you will fear." And, although the following has no scientific basis whatsoever, people such as Doreen Virtue who write about fairies today say that while one should respect the fairies, no one needs to fear them.

According to her, fairies will help you in many different ways if you ask them respectfully, and if they then deem you worthy of their help. They offer assistance in healing, career and job, relationships, finances, homes, and even ridding house and home of vermin.

Maintaining areas in the home or landscape that please the fairies—or at the least that do not offend them—can nudge fairy favor in your direction. In that case, fairies will not harm mortals in the vicinity, and may actually do nice things for them. This thought is believed to be the basis for fairy gardens.

Attracting fairies. Doreen Virtue says that to be worthy of fairy assistance, you must show respect for the environment, and at the same time earn the trust and respect of the fairies. Fairies are nature spirits, caretakers of the environment and all living creatures within it. They are mistrustful of humans and tend to stay out of our way. There are many ways you can show them that you are a friend, not an enemy.

Start by being environmentally conscious and by showing respect and kindness for animals. The more you believe, the more fairies will be attracted to you and your property, bringing with them good fortune. And of course you should express gratitude when they help you out.

To earn the trust and respect of fairies, you should:
■ Create a fairy garden
■ Respect the privacy of fairies

■ Garden organically, recycle, make compost, and don't pollute
■ Deal with pests humanely
■ Assist all birds, animals and insects in your garden by providing food, shelter and water
■ Leave small gifts and offerings for fairies to find, without expecting anything in return
■ Add music to your landscape for the enjoyment of fairies
■ Bring laughter and joy into your household and gardens
■ Talk to the fairies
■ Keep a small portion of your garden a bit on the wild side and all of it chemical free

WAYS TO SEE FAIRIES

It is said that fairies love the sound of children laughing, and certainly children see more fairies than do adults. Children have unfettered imaginations and a greater capacity to believe in fantasy, so it's easy for them to understand that although fairies may or may not be

Betty Earl

Tucked away in a secluded birch woodland, this rustic, twig-styled pavilion provides shelter and a comfy bench, a welcome retreat for a weary fairy. Photo courtesy of Jeremie Corp.

14

real, they are creatures of the otherworld and it is not always possible to see them with the physical eye.

Whether you believe or not, it is thought that though fairies are present year-round in the garden, there are certain times of the day and year when fairies are more active and more likely to be spotted by children, and some adults, too.

Timing is important in connecting with fairies. Beltane (the first of May) is traditionally a time when the curtain between the fairy realm and our world is at its weakest and that sultry summer evenings are usually the time for fairies to indulge in their favorite pastime of dancing and revelry. This tradition relates to our May Day celebrations. Nights of the full moon, the equinoxes, and the solstices are considered most appropriate for these dancing parties in secluded valleys, on sheltered banks near gurgling water, or within some concealed or hidden spot.

During these times, the light-footed sprites, filled with passion for the strains of unearthly music, glide in and out of their favorite dance figures the whole night long without stopping.

At the first glow of morning light, all fairies quickly depart for their homes hidden deep in rocky crevices, in knots and furls of old tree trunks, perched high in leafy trees, or within your fairy garden houses. Legends tell us that these sudden departures create a sound reminiscent of the loud humming made by bees swarming from a hive. It is believed that if they are seen by a mortal, it is just a glance and then they are gone. Fairies are shy, quick, and offended by uninvited mortal intrusions,

Maybe the only way for you to see fairies is to believe in their existence and wait for them to choose the time and place to reveal themselves. Success might be determined as much by your passions and feelings toward fairies as by the fairies' desire to be seen by you.

Whatever the past arguments and discussions, for the purposes of this book, I will simply acknowledge that the difference in spelling is the difference between the British English (faerie) and American English (fairy).

Top, a fairy sized wheelbarrow for transporting tools, flowerpots, and fruitful yields. Photo courtesy of Miniature Garden Shoppe. Bottom, a fun sign for a fairy garden. Photo, Betty Earl.

Is it Fairy or Faerie? The development of the term "fairy" is long, complex, and ambiguous. One theory is that faerie originally referred to the place where fairies lived ("fay" + "aerie") rather than the creatures themselves. Another theory is that the words fae and faerie came to English from old French, which in turn was inherited either from Latin or Farsi. Still others note that faerie was the spelling first introduced by the poet Edmund Spenser in his *The Faerie Queene* written in 1590.

And then there's the controversy of whether faerie and fairy are interchangeable terms. Some argue that faeries are the malicious and spiteful figures of legends and myths while fairies are the good, congenial and considerate small winged beings of more modern stories and tales.

Fairies are not known to have great home-building skills, so if provided with this whimsical, two-story cottage at the edge of the woods, any fairy would be thrilled to call it home. The stone path leading to the front door is lined with several "bushes" of thyme; while foundation plantings of blue-green sedum and green-and-cream variegated ground ivy add to the cool, calm color scheme. Dwarf conifers at the side of the house add height and some fragrance to this low maintenance fairy garden.

16

CHAPTER 3: CREATING A SUCCESSFUL FAIRY GARDEN

"It's easy to believe in magic when you're young. Anything you couldn't explain was magic then. It didn't matter if it was science or a fairy tale."
~~~~ Charles de Lint

The notion of fairies in the garden and gardening to please them isn't new. But the concept of fairy gardens as a hobby, or passion, certainly is, for it gives gardeners the opportunity to transform part of the garden into something magical. Whether they believe in fairies or not, people are inviting them into their back yards and gardens in ever increasing numbers.

The basic idea of fairy gardening is gardening in miniature, creating the illusion that tiny fairy creatures have taken up residence in your garden. This presents gardeners the perfect opportunity to throw their inhibitions to the wind, be creative, and let their inner playful child surface.

Fairy gardens are all about miniaturization. A fairy garden creates the impression of an endearing tiny world, of the sort and size that fairies might enjoy and inhabit. In fairy garden scale, a miniature fence has slats the size of a pinkie finger, a minuscule patch of thyme or moss suggests a lawn, a child's saucer full of water approximates a fairy pond, and a shard of flagstone the size of your hand becomes a patio. A fairy garden is a living, in-scale mini garden scene that is a source of satisfaction and joy.

Designing a fairy garden is the process of taking an assemblage of plants, a doll-sized fairy abode, and mini or micro accessories, rolling it all up into one creative tiny little scene, and laying it out there for the enjoyment of all. There is no right or wrong! Every fairy garden that is conceived, designed and planted with care, love, and attention to detail will attract and delight the garden fairies as well as its human visitors.

An outdoor fairy garden is more than just a darling house, pretty plants and cute accessories. To attract fairies it must also be eco-friendly, have a few "wilder patches" with hiding places for fairies to play in, and be attractive to butterflies and bees. Modern myths tell us that fairies are peaceful but mischievous ethereal beings that like to frolic and dance in gardens— and are also the ones responsible for knocking over tiny garden décor and trampling miniature garden plants when you're not watching.

Like many other hobbies, you can spend a lot or a little of your time and finances on it. Outdoor fairy gardens generally have a fairy house and numerous fairy-sized accessories. Google "fairy houses" and you will be amazed at how many sites have sprung up offering a wide range of fairy

accommodations, ranging from the somewhat small and crude abodes, to seemingly palatial mansions with hefty price tags. Many basic fairy garden kits are available, complete with amenities such as tiny arbors, fairy-sized benches, diminutive birdhouses and birdbaths, pebbles or stones, and even a bit of fairy dust. They may come with or without a container and potting soil.

You need not buy fairy houses or kits to get in on the enchantment. If you are creative, crafty, or appreciate a more economical approach, seek out items at garage sales, toy departments, and home décor stores that have fairy garden potential without being classified as such. Visit local garden centers and nurseries, many of which have a large section dedicated to this charming fad.

Go outside. Look around your landscape or take a walk in the woods and see what Mother Nature has to offer. Collect pine cones, acorn caps, dried moss, feathers, nuts, berries, pebbles and fallen bark. Using your imagination and a bit of architectural design, chic habitats for the other-worldly creatures can be had for virtually no cost. Be respectful of living plants, for fairies do not like anyone to harm them.

A few decisions will have to be made before you purchase or select that first plant, structure, or accessory. There are endless possibilities so don't rush the process. This can be done in stages over longer periods of time.

Fairy gardens are the ultimate dollhouses for adults, a source of satisfaction and joy. It is all about having fun. Just keep it small, simple, and uncomplicated, and I guarantee the fairies will appreciate your enthusiasm and reward your achievements.

A fairy friendly environment.

A fairy house and garden show fairies that you are congenial, hospitable, courteous, and friendly. Whether whimsical or deeply metaphysical, these creations allow enchantment to pass into our lives.

And though you may never feel that metaphysical connection, by providing them with this special habitat—just might show their gratitude by bringing you some luck and joy. They may also try to communicate with you when you least expect it.

Celtic lore has it that if you provide a fairy house and leave it in a secluded spot in your garden, the woods, a park, or a place of honor in your home, you encourage fairies to visit you. A belief in the existence of fairies helps, but even if you don't believe, this is an enriching way to spend time working on a project, especially with a child or a friend.

Always respect the environment, the privacy of fairies, and natural beauty. Fairies consider the fairy house and the space around it as sacred because of its function as a gateway between their realm and ours. Leave a crystal, a sparkly stone or button, or faux gold or silver inside your

fairy house as a sign of welcome, a sincere invitation for the fairies to move in. It is thought that leaving small gifts for fairies keeps them from playing mischievous tricks on you.

CHILDREN AND FAIRY GARDENS

Can anything be more natural than combining fantasy and children?

Gardening with your kids and grandkids is often a fun-filled family activity; but to be successful, it has to be enchanting and captivating for them as well. Some kids are naturally attracted to the idea of spending time in a garden but others might need a little more encouragement or a gentle push.

The magic of innocence. To a child, a fairy garden is a tiny world where magic happens. It's a place where their imaginations run wild, their creativity kicks into high gear, and their fascination with fairies and nature simply grows. With their firm belief in the existence of fairies, children easily accept the idea that fairies are hiding in secret places throughout the garden. Allow your child to build a fairy house out of found objects, then fashion furnishings from a pile of leaves, twigs, moss, acorns, and pods.

Imagine seeing the fairy garden through the eyes of a child. Feel the embrace of fern fronds towering over the fairy house, experience the gentle caress of a light breeze as it snakes its way to the fairy door at the base of the tree, and take in the enchantment of finding a fairy vainly gazing at itself in a puddle of water. Experience all over again that instant swirl of magic the minute a rosebud unfurls above the miniature arch, or the giddy joy in watch-

A miniature wood bench, tucked into a secluded spot between small boulders and purple-blue sedum, gives the fairies a peaceful spot for a bit of contemplation.
Photo courtesy of Landscapes in Miniature.

ing daffodil heads turn in sync with the sun above a miniature fairy ring. That's the secret of the fairy garden's appeal to children.

A fairy garden can suit the mysterious gardening hopes of many children while at the same time satisfy the gardening constraints of the adults helping them. Though small in size and easy to establish, a fairy garden can easily take on an immense life of its own in your child's eyes.

But if that garden is to be the perceived magical place for them to play in, it must center around their universal belief in fairies, their vivid imaginations, and the knowledge that there is no right or wrong in the project.

Choose your space. You can plan a fairy garden for whatever space you have, large or small, whether in the shade or sun, in damp woodland or a colorful flower bed. Even if you are limited by time, space, or financial considerations, with a little ingenuity on your part, your child can still enjoy the pleasure of a cherished and enchanted fairy garden made in a basket or container placed on the patio or deck, or even indoors.

Start by asking your child what plants and flowers they like and think will prove irresistible to visiting fairies. Take the time to discuss every plant, pointing out some very basic plant cultural requirements, admiring the striking color of the flowers and complimenting them on the various textures of leaf choices. This gives the young potential gardener a bit of ownership in the garden, making it more likely that it will be cared for, and possibly, well tended. Make the small area cozy and inviting to the child.

A little prep work on your part before your child or grandchild arrives can work wonders in the long run. Ideally, that special little nook for the fairy garden needs to be tucked away safely in a secluded spot. Fairies need to feel safe, secure and hidden, so a shaded area next to a tree or under a shrub is perfect. Though it's your garden and landscape, it is your child's fairy garden. Set up an area that fairies might flock to, but keep it within the scale that is right for a small child.

Make it easy for the child to settle upon your chosen spot by leaving a few clues ostensibly left by fairies, such as outlining the area with twigs or rocks. Plant things inside the area that fairies are reputed to like, making sure to include different sizes, shapes and textures of plants. Plant them so they look like they sprouted there, with small plants nestled below large ones, setting aside areas for fairies to play and soft places to sleep. Use bold colors and interesting plants, such as snapdragons, whose "mouths" little ones can open and close. Add daisies for daisy chains, fuzzy lambs ear for gentle stroking by little fingers, and creeping thyme and Irish moss for that magical forest feel.

A fairy garden is all about amazement, surprise, and fun, so stroll the garden together and "accidentally" discover the magical site. Gather nature's trea-

FAIRY GARDENS ARE GREAT CONVERSATION STARTERS AND THOUGHTFUL GIFTS. MAKING THEM IS AN ENGAGING ACTIVITY THAT CONNECTS KIDS WITH THE OUTDOORS, SUNSHINE, AND GARDENING.

This square container with a favorite fairy under a rustic arbor and wire vine (*Muehlenbeckia complexa*) at her feet is the perfect size for a side table or hostess gift. Photo courtesy of Jeremie Corporation.

sures—fallen bark and twigs, pebbles, rocks, cones, pods, and shells, if you live close to water—discussing what they may become in the fairy garden. Together make a fairy house or some fairy accessories like a tiny swing for fairies to enjoy. You can keep it simple or make it more complex. You can install permanent fairy doors and houses, or leave the structures as temporary items to be redone every time your child plays in the garden.

Whether your child truly believes in fairies or simply has a healthy imagination, this is a great way to introduce them to the garden. Fashion whimsical fairy doors set at the base of a tree or fanciful fairy houses surrounded by delicate miniature gardens. Give their imagination free rein by adding a few unexpected touches, like a tiny winged fairy peeping out of dense plants or some twinkling fairy lights.

Children delight in adding special items to attract fairies, such as sparkly things, acorn caps, and nut shells. Engage them in looking for signs of fairy presence by means of fairy gold (chocolate coins), fairy jewels (crystals) or fairy dust (glitter). Your child might even awaken to a mysterious disarray in the garden after a night of mischievous fairy merrymaking.

Add a few accessories such as a birdbath or a tiny pond for some water. Add miniature tree frogs, rabbits, and toadstools for the fairies to enjoy. Little girls will be in seventh heaven with the addition of a small metal arbor and a few intricately decorated metal tables and chairs. Miniature tractors, wheelbarrows, and windmills will attract little boys. Don't rush the project, spread it out over a couple of months for maximum enjoyment.

Little boys need to play in the dirt, too! Little boys and dirt go together like umbrellas in the rain, mittens in winter, and boats in water. Young boys never need an excuse to get dirty.

While some children always dream of fairies, some little boys may prefer something a bit more on the rugged side. In planning a fairy garden theme for them, there is always a way to combine their passion for dirt with their active imaginations. Consider helping them design a prehistoric dinosaur landscape, a

High above the play area in the Children's Garden in the Conservatory of famed Longwood Gardens in Pennsylvania, a handmade house for fairies hides on stilts in the lush foliage. Photo courtesy of Longwood Gardens.

20

dragon's lair, an archaeological dig, or a mini-construction site.

Gardening gets children outside, away from televisions and video games. Searching for fairy treasures is a way to have them take note of the little wonders that Mother Nature provides. And who knows? They just might be among the lucky ones who catch a glimpse of a fairy flitting happily through the garden!

YOUR OWN FAIRY GARDEN

Not all fairy gardens are made with or for children. If you are planning to create a fairy garden there are many ways it can be done.

First, think about whether it will be an indoor or an outdoor garden. Each has its advantages and disadvantages. Do you want to place your fairy garden outdoors in the general landscape or confine it to a container or window box? Or will it be indoors? If so, its container can rest on a tabletop, shelf or counter.

Outdoor fairy gardens created in a woodland setting under a tree or shrub or next to a stream or pond can be bigger, have more elaborate structures and accessories, and include a greater diversity of plants. They also offer room for future expansion or changes. Built into your existing landscape, a fairy garden allows for the illusion that your fairy abode is the real thing, inhabited by fairies that have moved right into your garden.

Another possibility outdoors is the use of weatherproof decorative containers like birdbaths, hypertufa troughs, whiskey barrels, or rusted wheelbarrows. If your fairy garden has wheels it can be utilized anywhere in the landscape, or

A beach scene is created with sand, clear blue marbles, and white picket fence, but it's the addition of a colorful Adirondack chair, dazzling surfboard, and flip-flops that steal the show. Photo by Betty Earl.

placed on patios, porches, or balconies. This allows the garden to be moved out of harm's way in inclement weather, for storage in protected places where winters are cold, or during large gatherings. The downside is that this just does not have quite the same mystique as a fairy garden hidden somewhere deep within the landscape.

Outdoor fairy gardens may be somewhat limiting in the choice of accessories, especially for those living in the colder climates, as many of these decorative items could eventually be damaged or destroyed by inclement or capricious weather. Since fairies are apt to be less active during the winter season, it is a good idea to overwinter the delicate accessories indoors, giving you—and the fairies—the opportunity for new arrangements next spring.

The formal home nestled among oversized urns and greenery is a delightful place for fairies to hang out. Photo courtesy of Jeremie Corporation.

In this charming vignette it is easy to imagine a fairy taking a short break, with wheelbarrow, garden tools, wellies, and mini hose left at the ready. Photo courtesy of Miniature Garden Shoppe.

Indoor fairy gardens, on the other hand, can be enjoyed year round, are easier to maintain, and are not affected by weather, but possibly are limited in the amount of space you can devote to them. They can be designed and planted as dish gardens, in baskets, terrariums, wooden boxes, or various sizes and styles of containers. It can be a project as simple as including some fairy-sized accessories within the pots of your normal houseplants.

Or you can use a series of smaller pots aligned in a row, each one holding a different combination of plants, aligned in a row on a windowsill or edge of a countertop. This way, your fairy garden can be easily rearranged or expanded with the addition of another pot. City dwellers with no garden or outdoor space or people with limited space and time can always find enough room on a shelf, countertop, coffee table, or window ledge to tend these miniature landscapes.

If contemplating an indoor fairy garden, decide where you will display it. The space and light available and the ambitiousness of the project will guide you in selecting the container and plants. If the only spot for your container fairy garden is on a coffee table with low light, your plant choices are limited. In a sunny area near a window, in a sunroom, or in an enclosed, insulated porch, the range of plants expands dramatically. The choice and scale of the plant material used in an indoor fairy garden is that much more important because the plants are what make the landscape believable. They do not need to

be difficult to grow. Creating a fairy garden that can be enjoyed inside at all times of the year gives gardeners and non-gardeners alike something beautiful to nurture throughout the year.

LOCATING YOUR OUTDOOR FAIRY GARDEN

Location is everything, even in the world of outdoor fairy gardens. Be it a sunny flower border, a cool shady corner, the herb bed, or a spot hidden at the edge of a stream or pond, the choice of location will prove vital when it comes to choosing your plants.

If your garden is small, the choice of location might be simple. If your garden is large, picking the perfect spot is harder. If you already have beautiful plants flourishing in your garden, the available space between these plants can narrow your choices.

However you choose your location, keep in mind that once completed, your finished fairy garden should give the impression that it's the real thing, happily inhabited by fairies.

Betty Earl

Deep in the woods, a new fairy residence in the beginning stages of landscaping. The fence is up as protection against critters, many rocks, dug up during construction have been collected and cleverly utilized, though the wheelbarrow tells us there are still a few more that need to be repositioned. Block stepping stones lead to an outdoor dining area, and the clever fairy has positioned two wrought-iron chairs near the entryway for rest and relaxation after a hard day's work in the garden.

Fairy gardens work best next to a tree trunk, under a bush, or alongside small scale plants with delicate, fine detail. The place for the fairy garden might be a secluded corner of the woodland garden or next to a moss-covered log. Let it be a surprise, something a visitor just happens to stumble across while rounding a bend in the path. How charming to encounter one nestled among ferns in the woodland or under the branches of a rose bush. What delight to spot one seamlessly integrated in the herb, rock, or alpine garden.

Choose a site that takes advantage of the best of the natural elements of your garden, such as plants, flowers and landscaping. Ideally it will be somewhat separate from other parts of the garden, but still in tune with the tone. Sheltered, out of the way places are appropriate, because dwarf or mini plants and miniature accessories such as fairy-sized wheelbarrows, watering cans, or arbors require protection from the elements and garden visitors.

PICK A THEME

You may have the mistaken notion that fairy garden *is* a garden theme. In one sense, you may be right, yet there are many styles and themes for fairy gardens. Narrow the scope of the little garden. The theme you have chosen will guide your choice of fairy houses, plants, and accessories.

Do you think your fairies might feel more at home in a beach setting or down on the farm? Maybe you feel they would rather play and frolic in a cottage garden or slumber deep within a woodland setting.

Maybe a gothic manor look is more your style, full of deep, somber colors, gargoyles, and accessories appropriate to that period. Or, how about an old fashioned flower fairy garden with a small cottage surrounded by a host of pastel flowers, a fairy swing and hammock, and a white picket fence.

If you have a pond or water feature in your landscape, a choice might be to convert a small section of a secluded edge into a maritime fairy dock. A waterfront beach house, small boat, raft, or float tucked at the shoreline would welcome sprites with inclinations toward water sports.

Or, why not a play on words using plants with fairy names? How about 'Apricot Fairy Queen' foxglove (*Digitalis purpurea* 'Apricot Faerie Queen'), or the 'Elfin' series of impatiens? Fairy snapdragons (*Chaenorhinum origanifolium*), 'Flower Fairy' series of geraniums (*Pelargonium*), roses such as 'The Fairy', 'Fairy Queen', and 'Lovely Fairy', 'Elfin' thyme (*Thymus serpyllum* 'Elfin'), Siberian Iris 'Fairy Dawn', Begonia 'Airy Fairy', and the miniature conifers *Chamaecyparis* 'Fairy Puff', *Picea glauca* 'Elf', *Picea glauca* 'Pixie Dust', and *Picea glauca* 'Pixie' come easily to mind. There are more, just search them out. The larger plants can be used in the background.

There is no limit to usable ideas, because you are the creator of your own world. You can make your fairy garden look like an Irish hillside, a French vineyard, a German river valley, a Cinderella castle, a Swiss mountain glade, or the Arizona desert. There are many attractive, petite succulent plant varieties available, so perhaps a desert garden full of different types of cacti and succulents surrounding an adobe house will be just the thing.

If your interests are rural in nature, a farm theme, complete with farmhouse, windmill, tractor, a horse, wheelbarrow, spade, and shovel can help you and the fairies enjoy farming. Or if spending time in your garden puts you into a contemplative mood, a Zen garden with stones, bonsai shaped conifers and dwarf shrubs, a bamboo hut, and carefully raked sand can bring out your meditative side.

If you are building this fairy garden with your kids or grandkids in mind, consider this project through their

Chamaecyparis pisifera 'Fairy Puff'. Photo courtesy of Iseli Nursery.

eyes. While a fairy princess fairy garden with stone castle full of pinks and whites and charming, delicate little wrought iron tables and chairs might entice your young daughter or granddaughter, it might bring your male youngster or grandson to tears. But a dinosaur themed garden full of moss, ferns, and other greenery can provide him with a fascinating forest where dinosaurs and raptors return from extinction to breathe and live one for another day.

If your child is into beasts and fiends and you have a patch of yard that remains wet and muddy despite your best efforts, a swamp garden full of carnivorous plants, imaginary crocs and wild pigs, twigs and small branches half submerged in mud might be just the ticket.

A construction site with stick logs and lumber stacked up waiting for the big rigs to move them may be another option for boys.

These gardens can go anywhere your and your child's imagination and creativity take you.

FAIRY HOUSES

Your fairy house is the centerpiece around which you create your fairy domain. Pick a house to fit the theme: a thatched-roof cottage for an English cottage garden, a shanty for a beach theme, or, if your theme is deep in the woods, you might dispense with the house completely and opt for a decorative fairy door and a couple of fairy windows mounted at the base of a tree as the fairy habitat.

Betty Mackey

Betty Earl

Top, thatch-roofed Primrose Cottage with its grand entrance is surrounded by colorful plants that would please any fairy. Above, this colorful terrace garden with tiny paving stones was entered at the Philadelphia International Flower Show.

Betty Earl

Fairy houses are miniature structures intended to attract fairies to a garden, a yard, your home, the woodland, or another place. They give fairies a place to be, to visit, or even to live in, if they so desire. Fairy houses are portals between their world and ours, used for entering into ours or escaping from it. When we interact with a fairy house it can open up a passageway into the fairy world and allow the child within each of us to come out.

For some, a fairy house is a way of saying they believe. And legends have it, that if people believe, the fairies hear them and are drawn to them, and that that singular act of belief is the catalyst that opens the door between the realm of the fairies and our world, and allows communication between the two.

Fairies need homes. Should your kids ask, and they usually do, you can tell them that, as a rule, fairies live wherever they can find a bit of shelter: deep in the forest safely tucked among gnarled tree roots, under stone outcroppings and ledges, behind tree stumps, or in the arms of a dense tree canopy. Though famous for their merrymaking and dancing, fairies are poor and somewhat lazy carpenters, preferring partying and laughing to working. Thus, they lead a precarious housing existence, and as the forest and landscape change with the seasons they travel from place to place in search of a suitable habitat. Fairies need someone to offer them a home.

A wrought iron arbor provides an enticing entrance to the stone steps leading to the cottage cleverly nestled among trees in a woodland garden.

These houses can take on a number of different forms. Fairy house designs can be as fancy or as simple as your imagination, time constraints, and financial considerations dictate. From the smallest and simplest ones to large, enchanted castles, thatched roof lodges, or elaborate dollhouse-like structures, pre-made fairy houses (there are many available) can be purchased online and at local garden centers or they can be conceived and hand-crafted at home.

Simple and charming shelters may be constructed with nothing more than pebbles, moss, feathers, shells, fungi, twigs, bark, and other natural materials. You and your young companions can have fun gathering them from your yard or in the woods or local parks. With imagination, little wooden houses can be created from materials you have on hand, or simple items that you can find at local craft or hardware stores.

Fairy house construction.

When building a fairy house, use only natural materials such as twigs, leaves, rocks, pine cones, acorns, dried flowers, moss and other such items. If you live near a lake or ocean, things such as shells, polished pebbles, small driftwood pieces, and seaweed can also be incorporated into the design.

Fairies do not embrace plastic houses or artificial flowers and including these items in a fairy garden design detracts from its charm. Mortaring together little tiles or stones to achieve a level area for the placement of miniature furniture or using glue, paint, wire, concrete or clay to stabilize or beautify a fairy house can only enhance the total design of the garden.

Live plants should never be picked for use in fairy house decorations, but rather respected and left to nature and the enjoyment of the fairies.

Available at most craft stores, small unfinished birdhouses make excellent base models for fairy house creations. Ingenious fairy house architects can skillfully design and renovate homes for fairies. For siding you can use cattail leaves or cover the walls with birch bark. Scales of pine cones or pine bark make excellent roof shingles, and grapevine tendrils, seed pods, moss, twig railings, and pieces of driftwood add interesting embellishments to the house.

Choose a spot with a good foundation—a tree stump, rock pile, or a mossy glen under a small bush—for it is helpful to have something firm on which to build upon, rather than start-

Betty Earl

A "mortar and stone" fairy house with seashell roofing, constructed by a young lady, takes center stage in the family's garden, proving that children can be quite innovative and resourceful.

ing with loose, bare dirt. Fairies enjoy seclusion, so avoid areas that get a lot of foot traffic or that might get flooded when it rains.

Typically, there is a door or entry for the fairy to enter and exit. Otherwise, the options and styles are limitless. Houses may be built into the ground or perhaps integrated into a tree. A pathway may lead to the entryway, or one might need to search to find a secret passage into the house. They may be simple in style or elaborate with many features. Some dwellings are so much a part of the natural environment that they may be hard to spot.

Fairies are not particular about color; however, you want the fairy home to blend into the environment, rather than stand out like a sore spot. Deep, dark colors work well, as do muted pastels.

When the little abode is finally finished, you can hang a little welcome sign in front of the house. Any fairy who happens to stumble upon this house will be more than happy to call it home.

Be forewarned: building fairy houses and designing fairy gardens is addictive. No sooner do you complete your first house than you'll be thinking about the next. You'll know you're hooked when you start building fairy gardens everywhere. As fascinating as fairy suburbia can be, refrain from turning your garden into a congested fairy sprawl.

FAIRY DOORS

A fairy door is a miniature door that is thought to provide fairies, elves, sprites, gnomes, pixies and similar wee folk an easy portal from their otherworldly realm to ours. The delicate paths through these ethereal mists have no pointers or signposts, so it's easy for a fairy to get lost and end up stuck in a tree trunk, a rock, or even the built-in entertainment cabinet in your home, searching for a way out.

You will be thanked for offering the fairies a doorway, leading to a path for a pleasant journey. Provide them with the opportunity to easily stroll between our world and theirs by attaching a fairy door to any surface in your home or garden. These fairy doors are magical things, and with their aid, fairies can stay close to you and your activities while still having an easy access portal to Faerie, their land of enchantment.

Fairies are tiny folk, too small to handle something as big as a human-sized door. Fairies need doors sized more to their small stature, and it's a wise human who provides them with these doors.

Whether you believe in fairies or not, children do. What better way to keep the magic of childhood alive than by making a fairy door. You can place these mini doors anywhere—on a wall or a baseboard, against a stone, a stump, base of a tree or high in its branches, in a child's playroom or bedroom—anywhere you want these bewitching gateways. Imagine the delight of a child upon discovering this evidence that fairies live in their or their Grandma's home or garden. See here! There's a door...there's proof!

If you attach one of these noteworthy doors at the base of your big human-sized door, or right beside it, you are extending an invitation to the fairies to come into your home and bring their good luck with them. Whether you believe in fairies or not, these Lilliputian doors are charming, a neat and nimble way to break the ice at your next party, and one of the best ways to put kids at ease in the company of adults.

A grand staircase comprised of wood pieces, with twigs for banisters, leads fairies to the second story landing of a multi-story condo located in a tree.

Betty Earl

Betty Earl

A portal into the enchanted world of fairies, a fairy door at the base of an old tree adds whimsy to the garden while enticing fairies to visit.

Only fairies and the wee folk can open the door between the two realms. Should you open the door, what will you see? Nothing more than the surface to which you've attached it. But think about this. If you offer fairies some treats of their liking or some sparkly gifts during a full moon, perhaps they will reward you by letting you see through the door into their world.

Bought or hand-made? Create a portal into the enchanted world of fairies with either a purchased door or one you've crafted yourself. These magical creatures fancy both kinds, so let your time constraints and imagination limit your decisions. Remember that fairies bring good luck to those who believe, but without a fairy-sized invitation—in this case, a small door—you will need more than luck to experience their magic.

Hand-crafted fairy doors can be a delightful and creative piece of playful garden art that captivates and charms any and all visitors. Always keep size in perspective. If the doors are too large, a small magical creature would find it hard to open without using some magic. And using magic to open and close doors is a waste of magic.

Unless a fairy door is built into a fairy house, which will then determine its size, here are some guidelines on size to help you. Though some fairy doors can be as small as four inches high, they should be no larger than eight inches tall and approximately four to five inches wide, including the door frame. They can be made of virtually any material: wood, stone, cement, plastic—even Popsicle sticks, if need be.

Fairy doors, available in numerous shapes and various styles, can be painted in all colors. Honestly, fairies are not choosy when it comes to color. All they are looking for is an earnest invitation into your world. If you are thinking of positioning one of these enchanted entrances in your home, then choose colors that match your décor. Decorate them with a few of nature's resources, a little whimsy, and an abundance of imagination.

For the perfect finishing touch to your door, add an intriguing doorknob. Fairies love sparkly things, so why not attach a doorknob made from a gleaming bauble, a brilliant crystal, or a piece of faux gold? This eye candy is sure to entice fairies to visit your world more quickly.

Remember, in the world of fairies, doorknobs are vital. A fairy cannot open a door without a doorknob, yet doorknobs often go missing. And though it is true that a missing doorknob can be nothing more than the work of a vandal or Mother Nature, it is also possible that you were visited by a smart celestial being. These intangible beings sometimes take doorknobs with them to ensure safe passage should they come upon a door without a doorknob. So if your doorknob is missing, chances are you were visited by a fairy. My suggestion would be to add another doorknob at your earliest convenience to give the next fairy the ability to pass unseen from one dimension to the next.

THE IMAGINATIVE FAIRY DOORS OF ANN ARBOR

While the college town of Ann Arbor, Michigan has many things to offer residents and visitors alike, none are more enchanting than the magical fairy doors that have popped up mysteriously at various downtown business establishments. These fantasy doors, built to scale for the "wee folk", can be found both inside and outside a number of institutions and the urban fairies, it would appear, have settled in quite comfortably.

These inventive miniature portals into imagined fairy homes, the brainchild of a local illustrator and "non-certified fairyologist," Jonathan Wright, are unsponsored, unauthorized works of creative public art that pop up around town and have captured the imagination and heart of the city.

The first to appear was a six-inch white wooden door with a carved jamb framed by miniature bricks outside Sweetwaters Café. Since then, many more have appeared at different businesses and the public library around Main Street.

These doors are built into the front of buildings, the sides of bookshelves, and even business entry doors. Even the Google Ann Arbor office sports a fairy door near the ceiling in its conference room. This door (left) has a glass panel with an aluminum frame and the fairies' Giggle logo in Google type and colors.

The elaborate detailing of each of these imaginative, minuscule doors is incredibly well thought out and complements the larger structures to which they are attached. One of the most visionary and artistically complex creations is found at the Ann Arbor District Library.

This fairy door can be found at the end of the "Fairy Tale and Folklore" bookshelf in the Youth Department. It is a small dark blue double door with a teal blue frame attached to the side of the library shelf. Surprisingly, it opens to reveal an entire miniature room which has been set inside a glued together and hollowed out collection of large books. There are windows on the spines of these books and when library patrons peek through they can see the lights and furnishings inside—a small table, decorated walls, and delightful furniture. A sign on the front of the shelf says it all: "Please do not touch. These books are out of circulation. Besides there may be someone living in them."

A sad note: not everyone respects fairies or welcomes them, for, unless it was the work of malicious gnomes, vandals have damaged the library's fairy abode. Repairs are currently un-

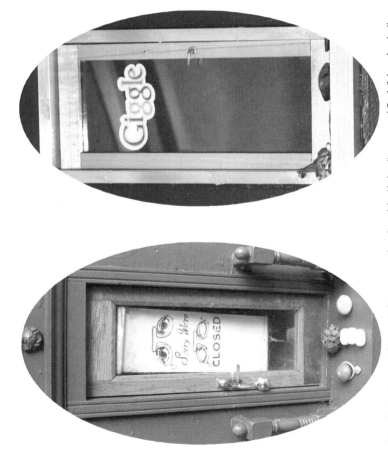

The fairy doors of Ann Arbor, conceived and built by "non-certified fairyologist", Jonathan Wright. About six inches tall, they are meticulously accurate and appropriately themed. Left, the fairy door to Peaceable Kingdom Gifts with it's own pull-down Open/Closed sign. Photo courtesy © urban fairies operations, LLC. Right, the fairies' own "Giggle" door in the conference room of Google offices. Photo courtesy of Google, Ann Arbor.

The imaginatively detailed teal blue fairy doors (above left) at the end of the "Fairy Tale and Folklore" bookshelf in the Youth Department (center) of the Ann Arbor Public Library. Patrons peek through the spines of the books (right) to view a miniature room complete with lights and furniture. Photos courtesy of © urban fairies operations, LLC. Below, one of Ann Arbor's first fairy door creations opens unto a circular stairwell. The complexity, intricacy, and fine detailing are amazing; the fairy door is only six inches high. Photo courtesy © urban fairies operations LLC, photo by Bob Foran Photography.

derway, and hopefully, it soon will be available once again.

The handmade fairy doors, for the most part, are generally placed low to the ground—the perfect height for viewing by delighted children and the young at heart.

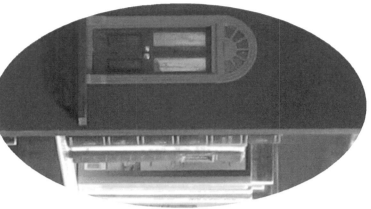

Chapter 4. Combining and Adding Plants and Accessories

"Where there is Joy, Laughter, and Color, Fairies will be found!"
~~~~ Author Unknown

Creating a visible connection among your site, your fairy house, accessories and live plants is the challenge. As in any regular-sized garden you have planted, scale, proportion, color, and pattern are important elements of design. To keep the composition interesting, vary the size, shape and texture of plants. If your fairy house looks formal, your landscape plan and accessories should be in the same mode. If it has a historical period, such as Victorian, let your plan and furnishing be compatible. If the door of the fairy house is six inches tall, a garden chair should be in scale with it, dollhouse size, and foliage should be tiny.

Once you have an idea of the space available for your fairy garden, it often helps to draft your plans on paper, playing around with different layout designs until you find one you really like. Keep in mind that a good plan not only will give you an idea of how your finished fairy garden will actually look, but it will also minimize frustrations and expenses associated with wrong choices. And though fairy gardens can be large, keep the design simple and interesting. Avoid adding too many elements to your design because it should not look cluttered or disjointed.

Examine the possibility of adding pathways, sparkling ponds or streams, mini patios, gazebos, and arbors. Design different layouts of pathways. Straight pathways work best for formal designs, meandering pathways look

Betty Mackey

A stone bridge over a fairy sized stream.

more natural and promote a relaxed state of mind. Try to get the feel for the difference in design between pebbles, tile, and formed brick sheets by drawing each style in the configuration you've chosen.

Consider the appearance of each garden feature or element in relation to your fairy house to see if they are complementary. Even if you have a specific idea of the ideal location of a pond, gazebo or arbor, test other options by moving things around. Evaluate whether you have enhanced the design with these changes or made it worse.

Look to your favorite fairytale films, books and art for inspiration. Note how the artists turn twisting roots, big stones, logs,and stumps into fantastic entryways or interesting doorways for fictional creatures.

Maybe the idea of enclosing your garden with fencing or walls appeals to you; or you might prefer to have the fairy garden blend into the surrounding landscape.

Betty Earl

An elegantly carved table and three benches perfect for afternoon tea or dining with friends.

It is said that fairies are attracted to water, so besides the addition of a pond—definite fairy eye-candy—possibly your design could be enhanced with a fairy-sized birdbath or fountain. If you've penciled in a stream, this is the time to decide whether you are ambitious enough to add running water, or instead will give the illusion of a stream or creek with colored marbles and glass. Is there room for a bridge? And have you penciled in a path to the bridge?

You can see how the design is ever expanding and changing!

This is the time to also consider some vertical possibilities. Yes, plants, arbors and gazebos give height to the design. But how about plant filled columns—a form of living sculpture. PVC pipes, drilled with small holes on the sides, wrapped in sheet moss secured with fishing line and planted out with baby tears, vinca vine, dwarf Mt. Atlas daisy (*Anacyclus* 'Silver Kisses') or sea thrift (*Armeria maritime* 'Victor Reiter'), for example, can add height, a form of living sculpture, and a spark of individuality to your design.

Consider amenities such as tables, chairs, and benches, which add a sense of magic and whimsy and are essential for attracting fairies. Include fairy sized hats, teapots, birdhouses, clay pots, fruit bowls, or other appealing miniature items for the same reason.

Scrutinize your topography. Would the aura of the outdoor miniature landscape be enhanced with the addition of valleys, hills, ridges or even some mountains? Would their addition complement your theme?

A quaint little area displayed in a trough for fairies to sit, relax and enjoy a sunny cottage garden. Photo courtesy of Miniature Garden Shoppe.

Keep in mind the location of the fairy garden as to plant choices: full sun, partial shade, or shade. Study catalogs for ideas and pencil in plants into the design noting size and their location. Once you are happy with the design, it is time to choose plants. You have a wide range of choices. Visit the local nursery or garden center, study plant catalogs, or go online to choose your plants, noting cultural requirements, hardiness zones and your affinity for them.

Consider the Internet for its wide selection of fairy garden accessories. Interesting small treasures can also be found in the dollhouse section of craft shops, flea markets, thrift shops, garden centers with fairy garden sections, discount stores, and hobby shops. When your purchases are complete, place the house, furniture, landscape features, and plants in their respective places in your fairy garden to test your design. This gives you an additional opportunity to experiment with different arrangements without stressing the plants or making a mess.

Study the arrangement from all angles. This is the time for thinking of any revisions, additions, or deletions.

If this is your first fairy garden, remember that creating one that meets all your criteria can take time. There is no need to rush, as it can be completed in stages. Go slow and enjoy the process.

Indoor Container Gardens

Pick your container. Be creative, but also realistic. Just about anything to which you can add plants would be suitable, but be sure it has enough depth to maintain soil moisture, and enough surface area to accommodate all the features you envision. Choose containers with proper drainage to prevent soggy roots. Containers with saucers work best, but if a wicker basket, antique terrarium, or your Aunt Hilda's ceramic bowl sets your heart aquiver, there are ways to get around the drainage issue. For containers incapable of holding liquid, such as woven baskets or wicker, consider lining the basket with plastic, then adding a layer of pebbles and charcoal before including soil. For the terrarium and ceramic bowl, omit the plastic, but add pebbles and charcoal before including soil. See Chapter 5 for more planting instructions.

Consider sketching your design on paper, moving and rearranging things until the design is to your liking.

Decide whether the container will be viewed from all sides or just one. If easily seen from all sides, the focal point, such as the fairy house, should be placed near the center, with shorter plants and accessories around it. If the fairy garden can only be viewed from one direction, the tallest item, be it structure or plant, should be located near the back with shorter plants in the foreground.

Create walkways and seating areas. Consider adding an arbor. Examine the visual differences among loose pebbles, stone, tile, and formed stone or brick sheets. Try to imagine dry-creek beds beneath a bridge, and patios built using mini-flagstones set in sand for your fairies to lounge on, and, if space allows, items like fencing and ponds. Though space is limited, the accessories you add will give your fairy garden that unique and personal touch.

Choosing plants well is vital here, and the next section includes specific suggestions. It's important to buy plants that fit to scale. You'll use only a few types, but they will generate a major impact on your design. Choose plants that are compact, or can be easily pruned, or look mature although they are miniature in height.

A charming fairy garden in a tub set on the porch by the front door lets visitors see a magical fairytale world complete with miniature plants, furniture, and accessories.

Betty Earl

Consider herbs, a fairy favorite. Most will stay small with just a little judicious trimming, are easy to grow, have the benefit of fragrance, and have trimmings for tasty additions to your cooking. Creeping thyme makes an especially great lawn for fairies to play in. Ornamental onion (*Allium senescens* 'Glaucum') can be turned into an adorable hedge. Lemon scented geranium (*Pelargonium crispum*) with its very small leaves can be easily shaped into a beautiful shrub or small tree.

Refrain from using too many plant colors, for the design can look jumbled. Rely on variations in height and texture for a more natural, cohesive look with just a few splashes of analogous color for punch.

And always, always use plants of similar light, soil requirement, and moisture needs together in the same container. If you wish, create a fairy community using several containers.

Plants for outdoor fairy gardens. Any type of plant can be incorporated into your fairy garden, but it is important to select plants that are in scale with it. They should stay small and not outgrow the garden space too quickly. This means using naturally dwarf or petite plants, not necessarily young plants.

For outdoor fairy gardens, be sure you select plants that grow well with the water and light you are providing—full sun, partial sun and shade, or full shade—as well as your gardening environment and hardiness zone. Visit your local garden center or

IF THIS IS YOUR FIRST FAIRY GARDEN, REMEMBER THAT CREATING ONE THAT MEETS ALL YOUR CRITERIA CAN TAKE TIME. THERE IS NO NEED TO RUSH, AS IT CAN BE COMPLETED IN STAGES. GO SLOW AND ENJOY THE PROCESS.

Nestled under trees in the front yard, this in-ground fairy garden retreat is perfect for relaxation. The colorful table and butterfly chairs provide a peaceful place for refreshment near the mini stream and garden. Photo courtesy of Landscapes in Miniature.

Top, *Erodium* species, center, chives in full bloom, and bottom, sea thrift, add soft color to any fairy garden. Photos, Betty Mackey.

nursery; those shops into fairy gardens will have a good working supply of suitable plants and knowledgeable staff. Browse herb and ground cover sections of big box stores and even floral sections of supermarkets.

Imagine plants in proportion to the fairies. Sweet alyssum can be a flowering hedge, Irish moss a lawn, trimmed rosemary a shrub, pruned boxwoods as indoor miniature trees, and those adorable dwarf conifers a mighty forest. Dwarf annual ageratum plants in full bloom make excellent hydrangea bushes. Trimmed boxwoods resemble rose bushes. Gnarled tree stumps, rock outcroppings, and decomposing fallen logs planted with a mosaic of mosses are like little jewels of enthralling color tumbling out of a dark background. Whether your theme is country cottage or dry desert, there are plants which, with a bit of trimming to expose some trunk, will be suitable elements in your design.

Thoughts on plants indoors and out. Even some weeds from your yard—for example creeping Charlie (*Glechoma hederocea*), outdoors a very invasive weed—with thoughtful trimming can be delightful indoors with gorgeous purple, trumpet shaped flowers, tiny round leaves, and bushy growth.

Some plants, though small in stature or delicate in appearance, are incredible fairy garden workhorses. Take angel vine (*Muehlenbeckia complexa*), for instance. Also known as wire vine, angel vine is a delicate looking yet extremely durable and vigorous climber, whose tiny little leaves on wirelike stems lend themselves perfectly to covering miniature arbors or giving a fairy cottage the ivy-covered look. But don't let its fragile appearance fool you: it's a tough little guy, a rapid grower in need of regular trimming to keep it in check. Ideally suited to our hot and dry winter homes, it is also forgiving to the gardener who forgets to water it from time to time.

With miniature or dwarf plants, especially when they are planted in containers indoors, keep this in mind: water by hand with a gentle spray only when the top inch of the soil is dry, trim more, and fertilize less. When the plant has grown so much that trimming is no longer practical, dig it out and plant it outdoors if hardy to your zone; otherwise, repot it into a larger container and enjoy it indoors.

Herbs and ground covers. There are many varieties of herbs to choose from, like chamomile, sage, thyme, and marjoram. Members of the thyme family alone can generate a handsome design of different colors, shapes and sizes. Some are suitable for both indoors and out. When choosing herbs, look for small leaves, short stature, tiny blossoms, and variegation or different shades of green in the leaves.

37

Tiny cups dusted with early morning frost. Photo courtesy of Landscapes in Miniature.

There are superb growers of tiny plants, tough little ground covers and perennials that lend themselves to being stuffed into tight quarters. An example is the extensive Stepables® product line from Under A Foot Plant Company. The beauty of many of these plants is that they possess a truly low, slow growth habit that only reaches an inch or so in height, ideal for fairy gardens. Even when in full bloom, many remain under six inches tall.

Another branded line, Jeepers Creepers®, offers perennials of low, spreading habit for sun and shade. Selections boasting colorful flowers or leaves are good selections.

Gardeners living in hot and humid Zones 7 through 9 will find that many of the plants listed for cooler zones will not thrive for them. Local nurseries and garden centers offer appropriate choices and recommendations.

When thinking of plants for fairy gardens, be creative. Think of using moss or thyme as a grass, creeping savory pruned as a small shrub or bush, and rosemary as a tree. Your fairy landscape looks best with short plants close to the fairy house and its accessories. Plants in the background and those outside the perimeter of the fairy garden can be more statuesque. They help to transition the scene into the adjoining landscape.

There are a myriad of low growing, ground cover plants available to you for planting in the fairy garden landscape. Let your design, location in the garden, hardiness, and plant soil and light requirements be your guide.

However, for outdoor container fairy gardens, the plant choice is more limited. You want your fairy garden containers to look like miniaturized versions of a landscape, not tangled or overgrown. When choosing plants, their size, aggressiveness, texture, and leaf or blossom colors are important design characteristics. Light and soil requirements and watering needs of the plant also need to be considered as you make sure your plant choices are compatible. If your container will have sun exposure most of the day, plants thriving in shade will not live long, so do not mix them with sun lovers. And plants requiring good, sharp drainage will rot when sitting next to water hogs. Consult your local nursery or garden center staff if you are unsure of a plant's requirements.

To get you started, here are a few excellent choices of plants for the landscape, but especially for outdoor container designed fairy gardens.

OUTDOOR PLANTS FOR SHADE AND PARTIAL SHADE

In these and other listings in this chapter, Z stands for the US Department of Agriculture hardiness zones. Locate your zone at www.planthardiness.ars.usda.gov. Plants listed here need some shade but still require some light coming through. They are grown in moist or normal soil. Zones are guidelines, as plant survival is affected by elevation, microclimates, wind exposure, temperature fluctuations, and geology.

Baby Tears (*Soleirolia soleirolii*) 2" high, moss-like creeping plant of threadlike stems with tiny apple-green leaves that drape over sides of pots give rise to mini white flowers in summer. For an exquisite golden carpet try 'Aurea'. Requires constantly moist soil, high humidity and good air circulation. Z 9-10.

Bugleweed (*Ajuga reptans*) 4" high, fast-growing compact plant forms low-growing clumps of tiny, shiny leaves in a bronzy-purple shade with short spikes of deep blue flowers in late spring. 'Burgundy Glow' leaves dappled in green, cream and smoky pink, 'Metallica' has

From top left, clockwise, creeping thyme, culinary thyme, Kenilworth ivy, violet, creeping Charlie, and mazus. Photos, top four, Betty Mackey, bottom two, Betty Earl.

glossy leaves in a bronzy-brown shade, 'Chocolate Chip' has unusual narrow foliage in dark-green overlaid with chocolate-brown tones in cooler months. All have short spikes of showy blue flowers in late spring. Z 3-9.

Corsican Sandwort (*Arenaria balearica*), 2" high, dense dark green mats of moss-like foliage with dainty white flowers in spring. Prefers cool shaded areas. Z 7-11

Golden Creeping Speedwell (*Veronica repens* 'Sunshine). 2" high, a flat carpet of brilliant golden leaves adorned with near white, pearl blue flowers in spring that brighten shady areas. Z 4-8.

Kenilworth Ivy (*Cymbalaria muralis*) 3" high, forms dense mat of tiny, medium green leaves on trailing stems. Tiny snapdragon-like lilac-blue flowers with yellow throats in summer. Does best in cool summers and moderate winters, detests high heat and humidity, Mini Kenilworth Ivy (*C. aequitrilobia*), 2" high, dwarf purple flowers bloom continuously throughout summer. Z 7-10.

Labrador Violet (*Viola labradorica*) 2" high, forms low tuft of green and purple-tinged with a profusion of small mauve-purple flowers throughout spring and summer. Z 3-9. Silver Korean violet (*V. grypoceras exilis* 'Sylettas') grown mostly for its rounded green leaves with incredibly intricate silver markings and veining resembling cyclamen with hot pink and purple flowers in late spring. Z 4-9.

Mazus (*Mazus reptans*) 2" high, features narrow, bright green leaves forming an attractive carpet, with tiny, purplish-blue, tubular, 2-lipped flowers with yellow and white markings appearing in small clusters in late spring through summer. There is a white form, too. Z 5-8.

Miniature Golden Sweet Flag (*Acorus gramineus* 'Minimus Aureus'), 2" high, versatile non-invasive, chartreuse-colored grassy-leaved sweet flag, with insignificant flower spikes and sweetly fragrant foliage. Z 5-7.

Miniature Hosta (*Hosta* cvrs) Those examples listed here are less than 7" high. There are many additional varieties to choose from. 'Pandora's Box' creamy white leaf with a slightly blue green margin; 'Shining Tot' has shiny, dark green foliage; 'Cheatin Heart' has golden wavy leaves; 'Yellow Boa' has narrow, undulating leaves of bright yellow; 'Teaspoon' has distinctive, rounded and cupped dark green leaves with a creamy margin; 'Stiletto' has wavy, narrow lance shaped leaves of green with a narrow white edge; and 'Peanut' has creamy yellow to white leaves with a dark green margin. Z 3-8.

Miniature Rush (*Eleocharis radicans*) 2" high, for that true grass effect. Deep green, grass-like blades give rise to tiny little flower beads in summer providing a perfect miniature lawn understory plant beneath similar moisture-loving plants. Requires consistent moisture. Z 7-10.

White Toadflax (*Linaria lobatus*) 1" high, soft-textured, small green shamrock-like leaves are topped with white flowers in spring and summer. Z 6-10.

OUTDOOR PLANTS FOR FULL SUN TO PART SHADE

These plants generally do best with full sun in the morning and protection from the hot afternoon sun. Should be grown in moist or normal soil.

Alpine Geranium (*Erodium reichardii*) 2" high, small, heart-shaped deep-green scalloped leaves, give rise to saucer-shaped white flowers with red veins blooming spring, then intermittently; 'Charm' sports medium pink flowers; 'Flore Pleno', rosettes of double pink blossoms with deeply colored veins Needs sharp drainage. Z 8-9.

Alpine Speedwell (*Veronica allionii*) 2" high, tight mat of olive-green foliage bearing chubby spikes of deep violet-blue flowers in early summer. Needs sharp drainage. Z 3-8.

Bearberry (*Arctostaphylos uva-ursi*) 2" high, prostrate low mat of leathery dark-green leaves and small, urn-shaped white to pinkish flowers in spring. Needs sharp drainage, moist to wet soil can lead to root rot. Prefers acidic soil. Z 3-7.

Blue Star Creeper (*Isotoma fluviatillis*) 2" high, flat carpet of tiny green leaves, smothered with starry, soft-blue flowers all summer long. Z 6-9.

Brass Buttons (*Leptinella squalida*) 3" high, interesting grayish-green fern-like foliage forms a soft, fuzzy mat with small yellow button-like flowers in spring; 'Platt's Black' has bronze-black foliage; 'Purple' has gray-purple foliage. Z 5-9.

Cinquefoil (*Potentilla* & cvrs) 6 "high—'Pleniflora' deep-green foliage with double yellow buttercup-like flowers in summer. 3" high—'Pygmaea' bright green mounds seriously covered with gold flowers; 'McKay's White' has creamy white flowers; 'Nuuk' has white blossoms. 2" high—'Mango Tango' has mango-orange and red bi-colored flowers in spring and autumn; 'Nana' has single yellow flowers. Tough as a groundcover, this one may be invasive. Z 3-8.

Creeping Speedwell (*Veronica repens*) 1" high, tough creeper featuring green foliage covered profusely with pearl white flowers in late spring to early summer. Look for varieties with golden foliage, such as 'Sunshine', or with pink or blue flowers for a bit of variety. Z 3-9

Dwarf Mondo Grass (*Ophiopogon japonicus* 'Nana') 2" high, ornate dwarf, deep green, grass-like foliage topped in summer with small pale lavender flowers. Z 6-10.

Dwarf Woolly Yarrow (*Achillea tomentosa* cvs), 'Lemon', 2" high and 'Aurea', 6" high, woolly, narrow and finely feathered, small gray-green leaves knit into a tidy, low growing mat with flat clusters of perky lemon-yellow flowers perched over soft-looking foliage in summer. Represents hot humid weather, is drought tolerant. Z 4-8.

When in bloom, the tiny pink flowers of alpine geranium are a perfect match for the pink chairs. Photo courtesy of Miniature Garden Shoppe.

atop wiry stems in spring; 'Victor Reiter' has compact gray-green tufts with a profusion of petite light-pink flowers; 'Nifty Thrifty' has a tight mound of variegated, green leaves edged in creamy white with bright pink flowers in mid-spring; 'Cotton Tail' has white blossoms. Needs dry, very well-drained, gritty soil. Z 5-9.

Silver Gem Stonecrop (*Rhodiola pachyclados*) 2" high, closely related to Sedum, clump forming, low growing succulent, excellent choice as fairy-sized cabbage in farm- or vegetable-themed gardens. Sprays of tiny white to soft pink flowers in summer. Z 3-9.

Turkish Speedwell (*Veronica liwanensis*) 2" high, small deep green leaves adorned with small bright-blue flowers late spring/summer. Needs dry, sharp drainage. Drought tolerant. Z 3-9.

Variegated Cotyledon (*Chiastophyllum oppositifolium* 'Jim's Pride'), 2" high, forms low mound of thick succulent green with creamy yellow leaves, upright stems with dangling chains of bright pea-like yellow flowers. Needs good drainage, will rot if kept wet. Z 6-9.

Woolly Turkish Veronica (*Veronica bombycina*) 2" high, a tiny mat of stunning furry white leaves covered with light blue flowers in mid-spring. Needs dry, sharp drainage. Drought tolerant. Z 5-8.

Betty MacKey

Dianthus species do well in sunny fairy gardens.

The visiting fairy steps gingerly on squares of Scotch and Irish moss. Photo and art, the Mackeys.

Irish Moss (*Sagina subulata*) 2" high, lush emerald green carpet of moss-like foliage with delicate white flowers in midsummer and **Scotch Moss** (*Sagina subulata* 'Aurea') bright golden tufts of mosslike foliage with star-shaped white flowers that bloom in spring. Z 4-8.

Pinks (*Dianthus* cvrs) 2" high, light gray-green, needle-like foliage with mostly fragrant, dainty blooms on short spikes in summer. 'Petite' has pink flowers; 'Tiny Rubies' has steel-blue foliage with little hot pink flowers; 'Rachel' sports double pink, very fragrant little carnation-like flowers; 'Royal Midget' has light green, soft spikey leaves with truly tiny, hot pink, semi-double blossoms; 'Firewitch' has deep-blue foliage, numerous scented, bright magenta flowers. Pinks tolerate heat and humidity, need dry, sharp drainage, and are drought tolerant. Z 3-8.

Rupturewort (*Herniaria glabra*) 1" high, used mostly for foliage. Tiny leaves create a dense carpet, insignificant green flowers; 'Sea Foam' gives an undulating carpet of tiny green leaves edged in creamy yellow with tiny spikes of creamy-yellow flowers in summer. Tolerates drought, fairly slow growing. Z 5-9.

Sea Thrift (*Armeria maritima* cvrs) 2" high, 'Rubrifolia' sports a round mat of stiff, grass-like, purplish-red leaves with small rose-pink flowers in tight round clusters

OUTDOOR PLANTS FOR SUN

Plant these in full sun in well-drained normal to dry soil.

Clumping Baby's Breath (*Gypsophila cerastioides*) 2" high, green-gray foliage with light pink flowers in late spring. Needs dry sharp drainage. Z 5-8.

Chinese Lobelia (*Lobelia chinensis*) 1" high, fast spreading perennial with small green leaves and light pink lobelia-type flowers all summer and fall. Needs sharp drainage. Z 7-10.

Creeping Thyme (*Thymus praecox*) 2" high. There are a great many selections of thyme, all with some degree of fragrance, of which we list just a few. A soft, aromatic low mat of dark green, shiny, little leaves covered completely with purplish-pink flowers in summer; 'Albiflorus' is smothered in white blossoms; 'Highland Cream' has variegated green with creamy gold-edged leaves and soft pink flowers; 'Nutmeg' has nutmeg scented green leaves, smothered by mauve-pink flowers; 'Purple Carpet' has mini dark green leaves smothered by bright mauve-purple flowers in summer; and 'Elfin' is a tuft former with gray-green leaves and soft pink flowers. Good drought tolerance. Z 5-8.

Woolly Thyme (*Thymus pseudolanuginosus*) has fuzzy gray-green foliage with occasional soft pink flowers. ***Thymus serpyllum*** 'Magic Carpet' has foliage which is dark green with bright-magenta-pink flowers. Z 2-9.

Dwarf Mt. Atlas Daisy (*Anacyclus depressus compactum* 'Silver Kisses') 4" high, gray-green lacy foliage, white daisy flowers in early spring and summer. Needs good drainage. Z 3-9.

Golden Bird's-Foot (*Lotus corniculatus* 'Plenus') 3" high, very adaptable to any situation, plants form a low, spreading mound of bright green leaves massed with small orange buds opening to golden-yellow pea-type flowers in early summer. Z 4-10.

Ice Plant (*Delosperma cooperi*) 3" high, glistening, succulent leaves with profuse magenta blooms. Tolerates heat, drought resistant. Z 5-11.

Miniature Wormwood (*Artemesia viridis* 'Tiny Green') 2" high, dense low mat of pale green foliage with interesting texture and aroma and tiny yellow summer flowers. Z 3-9.

Moneywort (*Lindernia grandiflora*) 1" high, light green leaves topped with unique looking blue flowers with white throats. Thrives in hot weather, needs sharp drainage, resents over watering. Z 7-9.

New Zealand Bur (*Acaena saccaticupula* 'Blue Haze') 4" high, blue-gray, fern-like foliage. Insignificant flowers followed by attractive mahogany-red burr-like fruit in late summer. *Acaena inermis* 'Purpurea' has ruby-red foliage in sun. Z 5-9.

Stonecrop (*Sedum* species and cvrs) 2" high, huge family of plants which form a low carpet of tiny succulent green leaves with golden yellow flowers in spring; 'Goldmoss' becomes completely covered with yellow flowers in summer, foliage turns red during cold months; 'Aureum' has

Here is a garden fit for any fairy. In a shady corner of the garden there is an entrance through a garden gate into a mini retreat surrounded by lots of delightful plants and a wrought iron fence, all in scale. Photo courtesy of Landscapes in Miniature

buttery-yellow tips in the spring and tiny golden star-like flowers appear in summer; 'Blaze' has bronze-green to beet-red leaves and small clusters of ruby-star shaped flowers; 'Baby Tears' has white flower spikes in summer; 'John Creech' has rounded deep-green leaves and small clusters of mauve-pink starry flowers. Aggressive, needs well-drained soil. Z 2-9.

Snowy Marguerite (*Anthemis carpatica* 'Karpatenschnee' (Snowcarpet)) 6" high, low-growing cushions of hairy, finely cut gray-green leaves and a profusion of long blooming, pure white flowers. Z 5-9.

Sweet Mountain Fleabane (*Erigeron trifidus*) 1" high, interesting wiry green-gray foliage forming tufts with daisy-like lavender flowers in early summer. Z 5-9.

Outdoor Plants
Prune these to resemble shrubs and trees.

Wild Petunia (*Ruellia caroliniensis*) 12" tall, light green leaves with showy blue or violet flowers that appear from May through September. Grow in part shade to part sun. Z 8-11.

False Heather (*Cuphea hyssopifolia*) 18" tall, highly branched plant with feathery sprays of foliage resembling Scotch heather with mini violet, white, pink or deep-rose blossoms. Best grown in partial shade. Z 9-11.

Broom (*Genista pilosa* 'Gold Flash') 6-10" tall, deciduous shrub is smothered in small golden yellow flowers in summer. Needs full sun, needs regular moisture, slow growing. Z 3-8.

Variegated English Boxwood (*Buxus sempervirens* 'Variegata') mature height 3'. Dense, mounded, compact, slow-growing form of common boxwood noted for its variegated foliage. Bright green, evergreen leaves have white margins. Tolerant of pruning and shearing, grows 3" per year. Best grown in full sun to shade in well-draining medium. Z 6-8.

Dwarf English Boxwood (*Buxus sempervirens* 'Suffruticosa') In 15 years, reaches 1' tall, slow growing. Its dwarf habit makes this ideal for shaping. Needs regular moisture, best in partial to full sun. Z 5-8.

Lithodora (*Lithodora diffusa* 'Grace Ward') 10" high, mounds of green leaves with beautiful, deep blue little blossoms in summer; 'Star' has blue flowers with a brilliant white edge. Excellent used as hedges, best grown in full sun to partial shade in well draining acidic soil. Z 6-8.

Conifers

Dwarf conifers come in an amazing array of delightful colors, classy shapes, and fine textures. Dwarf conifers are slow-growing, durable, tough, and trouble free plants, usually evergreen. This makes them easy to add to any outdoor fairy garden. Most garden centers or nurseries carry small conifers in vertical, spire and conical forms. You can order them online, too. The foliage ranges in color from blue and green to yellow and white. Choose among types with soft, fluffy needles, sturdy, small, stiff needles, fern-like foliage that curves and twists, or delicate needles that weep and drape.

Picea glauca 'Pixie Dust' is a dwarf, densely textured conifer, a tidy asset to any fairy garden. Photo courtesy of Iseli Nursery.

INDOOR (DISH) CONTAINER FAIRY GARDENS

To lessen confusion between outdoor and indoor container fairy garden plants, I'll refer to indoor container fairy gardens as "dish fairy gardens" or "fairy tablescapes."

Probably the best type of container for a dish fairy garden is an open, shallow one. The size determines how many or how few plants it will be able to support. It is best if there are drainage holes; however, if the dish or planter is deep enough for the addition of gravel and charcoal layers, you can use them. And though most stores have a good choice of planters, I prefer planters with more personality than just the round bowl look. Check out discount stores, consignment centers, garage sales, even your own basement for the perfect dish or container. If you have a beautiful basket that you've been hankering to put to good use, here's your opportunity. Just put a non-draining container inside of it or line it with plastic. Plant as you would any container without drainage holes.

Because dish fairy gardens generally have limited root space, plants tend to outgrow their space rather quickly. For this reason, it is best to choose slow growing plants. Additionally, be sure that you choose plants that have the same general light, soil, and water requirements. If you mix these, you are putting some plants at risk of an early demise.

Most garden centers and nurseries, and many big box, discount, and grocery stores have a good and relatively inexpensive choice of starter plants in 2 ½ inch pots. I am confident you will have no trouble in finding enough suitable plants for your project.

Tiny landscape gravel forms a path to the rustic arbor, set back from the edge of the container, creating the illusion of two separate rooms. Photo courtesy of Miniature Garden Shoppe.

INDOOR LIGHTING CONDITIONS

Look for plants that will grow well together. Here are three types of indoor lighting:

Bright Light: light from a southern facing window with bright light for most of the day.

Indirect Light: Light from an eastern facing window or the interior of a room with southern or western facing windows.

Bright, Indirect Light: The natural light in a room with southern or western facing windows or light from an all-day northern exposure.

PLANTS FOR BRIGHT LIGHT

African Violet (*Saintpaulia ionantha*) 2 to 8" tall, easy-to-grow plant comes in three sizes: mini, semi-mini, and regular. Clusters of purple, pink, white, rose or lavender flowers in single, double, ruffled or edged in a contrasting color are displayed over fuzzy dark green leaves.

Because it is constantly in bloom, it needs more sun than the average green foliage plant, so keep it closer to a southern facing window. Remove spent flowers promptly. Wait till the surface of the soil is dry before watering. Prefers being watered from the bottom or directly on the roots of the plant to prevent leaf browning from water spots.

Dwarf Mondo Grass (*Ophiopogon japonicus* 'Nana') 2" tall. A miniature grass-like plant with stubby, grass-like green leaves and small, lavender-colored blossoms in summer. Water when dry.

Lace Flower (*Episcia dianthiflora*) or Flame Violet (*Episcia cupreata*) 6" tall, trailing relatives of African violets. Lace flower has dark-green leaves and white flowers with fringed petals. Flame violet's leaves are a combination of green and coppery brown, often with light green or silver veins, with a metallic sheen and red tubular blossoms. It prefers evenly moist soil during active growth, at other times, you can allow it to dry between waterings. It enjoys high humidity.

Maidenhair Vine or **Wire Vine** (*Muehlenbeckia complexa*) Outdoors, this is a vigorous vine. Indoors, where roots are contained, it is not aggressive. Popular with fairy and miniature gardeners for training up miniature arbors or trellises, but needs periodic trimming to keep in bounds. Wire vine is a delicate looking yet tough plant with tiny dark colored stems covered with tiny green leaves. Water when dry.

Panda Plant (*Kalanchoe tomentosa*) 6" and taller. Lovable plant grown for fuzzy, silvery leaves with reddish brown tips. Allow the soil to dry a bit before watering, and avoid getting water on the leaves.

Pilea (*Pilea* species) a group of upright, bushy and trailing plants, that are very easy to grow. Some of the more popular ones include 'Moon Valley' (*P. mollis*) with deeply grooved, bright green leaves with copper veins and tiny yellow flowers in summer. A compact and bushy plant, it should be pinched regularly to keep it from getting leggy; Artillery Plant (*P. microphylla*), with feathery stems and very tiny pale green foliage resembling that of a fern; Creeping Charlie (*P. nummulariifolia*), small and compact, with green, quilted leaves are only half an inch across, with an attractive, trailing habit; and *Pilea depressa*, a creeper with tiny, round leaves on rigid stems. Most pileas prefer to be kept on the dry side, so water only when it is dry or nearly dry.

Polka Dot Plant (*Hypoestes phyllostachya*) 3-12" tall, an adorable very colorful plant available in pink, white, silver and rose freckles, spots and blotches over dark green leaves. They tend to get leggy with age, so keep them pinched and cut back hard when they crowd their space. This plant prefers moist, but not wet, soil, and higher humidity.

Shamrock Plant (*Oxalis regnellii*). 6-8" tall, attractive clover-like green leaves with white flowers. Moist soil.

Succulents (many choices here including *Crassula*, *Echeveria*, and *Sedum*) can withstand a good deal of neglect, making them perfect for inexperienced gardeners. Use cactus soil. Water only when soil begins to dry out.

Waffle Plant (*Hemigraphis* 'Exotica'), 6-9" tall, ruffled or puckered, glossy maroon-purple leaves above and wine red beneath with small white flowers in terminal spikes in late spring early summer. Needs consistently moist soil.

The charming and easy-to-do fairy garden in this hypertufa container features a playful collection of contrasting succulents. Photo by Betty Earl.

PLANTS FOR BRIGHT INDIRECT LIGHT

Baby Tears (*Soleirolia soleirolii*) up to 6" tall. Tiny, round leaves cascading down slender, fragile stems. Has a low, spreading habit, moss-like appearance. Needs constantly moist soil. Perfect for those who like to fuss with plants. Prune it to your heart's content.

English Ivy (*Hedera helix*) Varied height. Attractive foliage, easily trimmed or trained over miniature arbor. 'Glacier' has variegated bluish-green with gray-green and white leaves; 'Needlepoint' has deeply lobed, medium green leaves. Needs evenly moist soil and higher humidity.

Ferns. This is a huge family of houseplants (Button, Curly Bird's Nest, Maidenhair, Club Moss, Plumosa, *Pteris*, to name a few) but they all need roughly the same care: preferably a humid environment, moist but not wet soil and medium light.

Mosaic or Nerve Plant (*Fittonia albivenis*) 2-6" tall with intricately veined, deep green leaves. The most typical veining is silver-white, but red, pink or all white also easily found. 'Frankie' has almost pink leaves with green edging; 'Red Anne' has wide bands of pinkish-red veins. This one needs evenly moist soil and can collapse when dried out, and also needs higher humidity.

Peperomia (*Peperomia* species) 6-12" tall with leaves that vary from heart-shaped to elongated teardrop-shape and from deeply waffled to smooth and waxy green leaves. 'Pixie' and 'Princess Astrid' (6" tall) are commonly available, as is 'Watermelon' which has distinctive silver and green striped foliage. Other good choices: Japanese peperomia has rippled texture, pinkish red stems; 'Jayde' has shiny teardrop-shaped green leaves; 'Rainbow' has red stems and elongated leaves marked with a broad band of cream; 'Red Luna' has reddish, deeply crinkled waxy leaves; 'Metallica's leaves are marked with silvery gray. Water when soil is on the dry side.

Spikemoss (*Selaginella kraussiana*) 2-6" tall. A cousin of ferns, spikemoss forms a low creeping mat of feathery green or yellowish leaves. **Golden Spikemoss**, *Selaginella* 'Aurea', has leaves of bright chartreuse yellow, providing interesting color contrast in planters. Needs consistently moist soil.

Strawberry Begonia (*Saxifraga stolonifera*) 6-9" tall. Small plant with rounded leaves in a loose rosette; plantlets attached by small runners, green leaves covered with fine hair with silver markings. Plants sport white flowers in spring and summer. This can grow indoors or out and prefers moist soil.

PLANTS FOR SHAPING INTO TREES OR SHRUBS

When considering plants to be used in dish fairy gardens as trees or shrubs, one easy way to choose appropriate plants is to look for plants designated as bonsai plants or bonsai-appropriate plants.

Betty Mackey

Betty Mackey

Edward Mackey

Top, strawberry begonia; center, jade plant; and bottom, fernlike Spikemoss.

(Top) For Northern gardeners, removing fragile fairy accessories might be a necessity; however, the remaining hardy plants in the hypertufa will bring four season interest. (Bottom) A simple design, enhanced by lush plantings, is the perfect spot for a cup of tea. Photos courtesy of Landscapes in Miniature.

THESE DO BEST IN BRIGHT LIGHT:

Begonia. (*Begonia partita* 'Little Hippie') quickly forms swollen tree-like base with small, pointed leaves and white flowers during summer months. Needs moist but not wet soil.

Calico Plant (*Alternanthera* cvrs) 6-30" tall. Easily trimmed, with richly colored leaves in purples, oranges, reds, bronzes, purples and yellows. Trimmings can be easily rooted and grown outside as annuals. Prefers moist soil.

Jade Plant (*Crassula argentea*) Any jade plant will work; however 'Mini Jade Fuzzy Leaf' is the smallest leafed, shortest jade plant I have found. Maturing at 6-8 inches, this is a perfect addition to an indoor landscape. 'Nana', another small Jade, has round green leaves with red hues. 'Nana' is a cascading plant, reaching 8 inches at maturity and can be trimmed to resemble a weeping tree. Water when soil is on the dry side.

Dwarf Mirror Plant (*Coprosma kirkii* 'Variegata') 12" tall. Tiny, densely branched stems with small waxy cream-margined gray-green leaves. Inconspicuous flowers can give rise to attractive, translucent white berries. Very tolerant of moist soil conditions.

English Boxwood (*Buxus sempervirens* 'Variegata') is a dwarf, slow growing, variegated boxwood that prefers moist but not wet soil.

Greek Myrtle (*Myrtus communis minima*) is a tiny shrub-like plant with fragrant thin, stiff stems and tiny, pointed, medium-green leaves sporting solitary white flowers in summer. Normal to moist soil.

Hebe (*Hebe buxifolia*). 'Patty's Purple' and 'Amy' are good choices. Hebe is a small shrub with glossy, boxwood-like leaves. Loads of small lavender flowers grow on small spikes for long periods at a time. Water when dry.

Japanese Holly Fern (*Cyrtomium falcatum* cvrs), which grows 19-24" tall, has fronds that resemble holly leaves with a glossy, deep green, leathery appearance. Needs moist but well drained soil.

CACTI AND SUCCULENTS

There are many different shapes and sizes of succulents, including miniature Haworthias, Crassulas, Sedums and Aeoniums that are slow growers with low maintenance demands. Taller succulents can be trimmed to stand in as trees and give height to a fairy garden. Cacti and other succulent plants are available at most nurseries, garden centers, big box stores, and online sources throughout the year. However, the diversity of available plants varies greatly at different times of the year and in different parts of the country. My best advice is to check locally first, then if you are not satisfied with the selections available, turn to online sources.

FAIRY GARDEN ACCESSORIES

Now the real fun begins! Apart from the plants, there are small accessories that should be part of an ideal fairy garden. Fairy-friendly miniature café tables and chairs, benches, fountains, and fireplaces all add to the charm of your garden. Swings and hammocks give the fairies a place to lounge and linger.

On a bed of creeping thyme add a bench, a tiny birdhouse and a birdbath and you have a secluded place for fairies to hang out. Hang a toy tire swing from a nearby branch, place a tiny boat tied off by the pond or dock, or scatter tiny mushrooms in the woodland setting.

Little boots, watering cans, straw hats, fairy-sized golf clubs, wheelbarrows and bicycles, gazing balls, garden hand tools, and colored stones and crystals in a water-filled birdbath are novelties for creating adorable vignettes.

Since fairies are fond of shiny things, entice them by hanging strands of shiny beads, crystals or mini-mirrors from branches as "fairy bait."

Take your time selecting fairy-sized accent pieces to complement your house and theme. That intricately detailed, white wrought iron table and accompanying chairs would look jarringly out of place if your theme is a woodland garden. A rustic set of benches or chairs made from twigs or wrought iron might be the better choice.

It's tempting to go overboard with ornamentation, so approach all additions with a light hand. A garden hat carelessly left behind on a chair with scattered mini pots, gardening boots, and watering can nearby, or a fishing rod leaning against a tree beside a pond is all it takes to make a garden look realistic.

A couple of fairy-sized bells or a single wind chime that magically tinkles as fairies scoot by, two enticing chairs by a Lilliputian pond, or a single table and chairs set on a small patch of moss presents a far more mesmerizing scene than a hodgepodge of accouterments in the same space ever could.

As gardeners we appreciate our tools, so essential when working in the garden. A shovel left leaning up against a wheelbarrow loaded with empty mini pots next to a fenced in vegetable garden, with a hose at the ready, gives the illusion of activity behind the scene. Succulents planted in sand, an Adirondack chair, a pair of flip-flops, seashells, starfish, and a surfboard stuck upright in the sand reminds us of balmy weather activities.

A light sprinkling of snow keeps fairies inside with a glass of wine by a warm fireplace. Photo courtesy of Landscapes in Miniature.

Fairies have a reputation for being notoriously vain; hence, most well-thought out fairy gardens include a reflecting pool. If there is no space for a pool, fairies can admire their reflections in a diminutive gazing ball.

When working with fairy gardens and sprites, why not stage a scene? Who could resist cookies and a cooling cup of fragrant herbal iced tea or fairy wine? Set out some tea pitchers, tumblers, and fairy-sized dishes on a decorative table in the shade, and the wee folk will flock to your garden.

Keep a few surprises by tucking in some accessories in out-of-the-way places, noticeable only upon close inspection—a smile waiting to happen for those who stumble upon them.

Betty Earl

Though fairies typically are uninterested in work, this garden-loving fairy keeps his tools ready for a productive day in the garden.

All of these are just a small sampling of the countless fairy garden furniture and garden accessories available at garden centers, hobby stores, arts and crafts shops, and online outlets.

Not everything need be store-bought. With a bit of imagination, grapevines, small twigs, mosses, seeds, pods, hemlock cones, and leaves can be used to create whimsical accessories, giving your fairy garden a personal touch. A lotus pod stuck into the ground then covered with sheet moss, combined with wood stumps for benches and chairs, makes for an adorable fairy-sized dining table set. A lovely seating area can be had with chairs cut out of branches with a stump for an end table, or with flat stones, pebbles, and a glue gun. Popsicle sticks cut in half crosswise and wired together make excellent fences.

In your hands, large upholstery tacks can easily be turned into mushrooms by giving the rounded caps two coats of deep red acrylic paint, then adding small dots of white paint for that toadstool effect. Finish with a coat of sealant and you have enough mushrooms for a fairy ring or for a little color on the forest floor. Just remember to let each coat dry before applying the next one. In a pinch, deep red nail polish will do the job quite effectively.

A sheet of mini, mesh-mounted glass, stone, brick, or pebble tiles available at most big box or tile outlets can be cut to size for outstanding pathways or patios. Once laid on the soil, all that is needed to ground it to your design is black sand brushed into the cracks as mortar. Another, probably easier method would be to gently water the sand into the cracks, but here care must be taken not to over water an indoor fairy garden.

A simple sign to welcome fairies can be made easily by cutting a picture or saying from a catalog or magazine, encasing it in plastic then stapling it to a popsicle stick. A cracked or broken colorful flower pot can gain new life by using the broken colored pieces to make a patio for your miniature garden.

The dog, yellow chairs, tiny pots, and gazebo are not dwarfed or overwhelmed by the plants in this container garden. Photo courtesy of the Miniature Garden Shoppe.

ADDING FAIRIES

If actual fairies are a bit scarce in your garden, you might consider those that can easily be found at your local garden center or nursery or from online sources. It depends on how much you want to leave to the imagination. Some people choose to include miniature fairy statues in their garden, while others prefer to opt for fantasy and hope that real fairies will one day visit and decide to stay. Some don't believe in fairies, but for others, these nature sprites are much more than a myth. Some believers feel statues may offend and keep real fairies away, while others see statues as a way to entice them and make them feel at home.

For added charm, consider inviting the celestial Cicely Mary Barker Flower Fairies to your fairy garden. Associated with specific flowers, the small, delicate statuettes are available in a variety of glimmering, winged, diminutive forms, resplendent in delightful petals and leaves. Since it's impossible to count on real fairies to make an appearance, you may want to place them in the foliage, peeping out from nooks and crannies, sitting on benches, walking down a pathway, looking at their reflections in the water, or radiantly emerging from a cluster of cheerful blossoms.

Consider the available space and the house and accessory proportions when making these decisions, for it would be odd and could even offend the fairies if the statues tower over the miniature landscape.

Group a few round stones in a circle for a campfire, add a few small, dark-bark twig pieces for a burning wood effect. Then cut small branches in one-inch lengths, chop them lengthwise into four pieces, stack them together in a small pile near the "campfire" and you have created the perfect venue where fairies can warm themselves on cooler nights, toast marshmallows, or enjoy some s'mores.

It only takes a large seashell for the tub, four smaller spiral shells for legs, and a glue gun to make a functional fairy bathtub. Nigella pods and tiny grapevine spirals can easily be turned into ambrosial fairy tea sets, and a flat piece of wood and a bit of wire into an attractive swing. Arbors and trellises can be had out of small pieces of wood; while a flat piece of bark, twigs and sheet moss in creative hands can easily morph into a canopy bed any fairy would love.

Even a young child can glue a piece of bark to a flat stone for a fairy tea table.

Betty Mackey

Legends tell us that fairies are attracted to water. Stepping out on a wooden springboard, fairies can try their hand at fishing or simply gaze at their reflections in the lagoon.

Betty Earl

CHAPTER 5. GARDENING WITH THE FAIRIES

"There never was a merry world since the fairies left off dancing..."
~~ John Seldon

Every civilization, society, and culture has a wealth of fairy myths, legends, and stories told and cherished by countless generations. They fire our imaginations, attempt to explain mysteries, note cultural traditions, or describe how long-ago people coped with crisis and conflict. Some of the more common ones are listed below.

What kind of garden do fairies like best? Whether you believe in fairies or not, questions arise as to what kind of flowers and herbs would be most likely to attract a fairy, or better yet a family of fairies, to your garden. Be sure to incorporate at least a few of the flowers most attractive to fairies within your landscape or indoor fairy garden, thus providing a welcoming haven for them.

We know that fairies are captivated by a garden full of colorful plants and flowers in which they can frolic and play. They are shy creatures, very protective of their privacy. They will be attracted to a patch of the garden left wild and full of secret places, hidden nooks, or knots and gnarls and hollows of trees to hide in.

We learn that fairies have a particular attraction to herbs, enjoy plants and flowers native to the area, and are especially fond of plants that attract wildlife, from birds and bees to other insects and animals.

Caring for wildlife is also important, for fairies are said to be the guardians of nature, and would gladly flock to a garden tended by a mortal who nurtures plants, animals, birds and insects with equal care and concern.

Fairies are infinitely playful. A garden full of fairies is not a quiet one, far from it. It is a world where fairies sing and dance, laugh while playing merrily on twisted twigs and branches, and gleefully frolic amidst fragrant blossoms. Believing in these otherworldly sprites is believing in a world where making spells, disappearing at

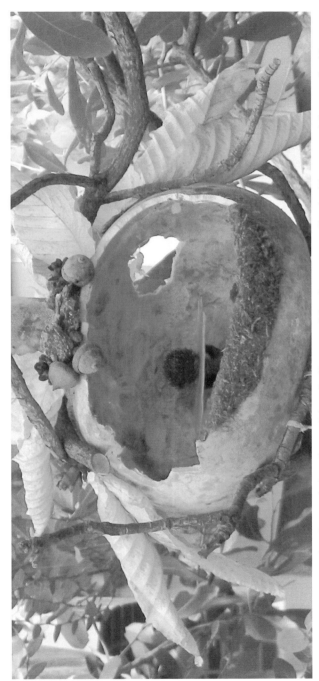

This fairy house is made of natural, found materials: a hollow gourd for the structure, lined with moss and decorated with twigs, acorns, and beech leaves. Note the little table. It hangs in the Children's Garden. Photo courtesy of Longwood Gardens.

51

will, or flitting from place to place is as natural as breathing.

Certainly, a mini wildflower meadow is a fairy haven, and it's a wise gardener who plants a variety of cottage flowers providing a range of colorful blooms from spring through fall (or year-round if you live in a warm climate) for the fairies to enjoy. Fairies prefer gardens that are as natural as possible, so keep pesticides to a minimum.

A SAMPLING OF FAIRY LEGENDS

Most fairies are offended by a spoken thank you. Leave them food or trinkets as thanks. Once offended, they will leave and never return.

Mortals are entranced by the beauty of dancing fairies, but watching them is a dangerous act. Should the fairies lure and then catch a mortal, the mortal would be forced to dance all night to complete exhaustion.

Fairy music is more melodious than human music, and myths tell us that many European fiddlers and pipers learned their songs from the fairies. Even the popular song, *Londonderry Air*, was thought to be a gift from the fairies. However, it was dangerous for young girls to sing all alone by a lake, for the water fairies would draw them down to sing with them under the lake and their families would never see them again.

"Elf locks" are tangles fairies put in the hair of sleepers for their own amusement.

As for protective charms, cold iron is the most familiar, but other things are also detrimental to the fairies: wearing clothing inside out, running water, church bells, and, of all things, bread. Varying from stale to hard tack to a slice of fresh home-made, bread was one of the most common of protections against fairies, typically employed by putting a piece of dry bread in one's pocket before venturing outside.

It was believed that fairies could be seen when viewed through a small stone or shell that

The garden of this fairy castle includes plants and features that fairies love, such as water, herbs, and paved areas for dancing and music.

had a hole worn through it from rushing water, or by bending a grass leaf into a circle and looking through it.

Fairies love milk, but if you lace it with pearlwort (*Sagina subulata*) it will render the fairy powerless against humans. Tossing a hot coal into the butter churn will keep fairies from stealing the butter.

On Fridays fairies have special power over all things and primarily on that day they select and carry off young and beautiful mortal girls as brides for the fairy chiefs.

Fairy doctors are generally females, most often old women, curing by charms and incantations passed down through generations and with herbs, of which they have a surprising knowledge.

Fairies are very vain, and love looking at their reflections in pools of water. However, they hate mirrors. Hanging mirrors near the entrance to your home will ward them off, but hanging them in your gardens will attract them.

Betty Earl

Fairies are attracted to pretty rocks and stones, chief among them, staurolite, fluorite, peridot, jade, and their favorite, the emerald.

Some legends note that if during a full moon you walk nine times around a fairy rath (circular fortified settlements built mostly during the Iron Age), you will find the entrance to Sifra, the jeweled home of fairies. Other myths claim it had to be the sacred tree, not a rath. But beware of eating fairy food or drinking fairy wine, for if you indulge you will never be allowed to leave.

ARE THEY THERE?

So how do you know if you are gardening with fairies?

It is really quite simple! Legend tells us that fairy voices echo within the gentle whispers of a breeze, their faces peer at us from the trunks of gnarled old trees, and the ripples on an otherwise still pond are nothing more than fairies playing. We catch glimpses of them everywhere: in the fleeting movement of light, in the midst of ravishing blossoms, in the musical notes of a rushing stream, and in the playful antics of butterflies and fireflies, their favorite playmates.

It is believed that fairies are present in all gardens in some form, as there are fairies tending plants everywhere. And with luck, it may even be possible to see the fairies who have taken up residence in the garden you've created for them.

We can't explore the universe or solve age-old mysteries about legendary beings, but we can use our imaginations to create a tiny, inviting world where we can all play with fairies.

FLOWERS AND PLANTS FOR FAIRY USE

The plants used in a fairy garden should entice the winged sprites to come, take a peek at your fairy garden or the rest of your yard, and, finding plants that meet their needs, stay.

Over the years, a number of plants became associated with fairies, either as a good choice for warding them off or curing the diseases they were believed to cause, or as plants which were special or sacred to fairies.

Rosemary, one of our beloved herbs, can be used to entice fairies to your garden. A tender perennial, rosemary can be used outdoors in mild climates, but in regions of the country which experience frost, hard freezes, or snow, it is best to relegate it to indoor gardens. Myths from Sicily where it grows wild note that fairy babies sleep among its fragrant blue flowers.

Low-growing **ground covers** provide an open area inviting fairies to linger; and the vast **variety of thymes** comes to mind whenever fairies are mentioned. Tiny creeping thymes and wooly thymes which spread over rocks or dirt provide fairies with a soft place to sleep or dance the night away. Cushions and coverings of **true mosses** or mossy patches of **Irish and Scotch moss** are ideal for fairies.

Some gardeners try to entice fairies to the garden by providing fairy statuettes looking happy and comfortable.

Betty Earl

53

Bell shaped flowers have long been associated with fairies. For the latest in haute couture, fairy lore holds that they are used to make parts of their clothing, such as hats, skirts and petticoats, and as cradles for fairy babies, little boats or even inventive whole houses for the tiniest wee folk.

Hollyhock (*Alcea rosea*) blossoms (pink is a favorite) make stupendous dancing skirts, **nasturtium** (*Tropaeolum majus*) leaves make excellent umbrellas, and **sweet peas** (*Lathyrus odoratus*), **columbines** (*Aquilegia* species), and **bells-of-Ireland** (*Moluccella laevis*) are just the thing for the latest in fairy bonnets.

Though tall, elegant **foxgloves** provide fairies with thimbles and caps; they are also the perfect spot for fairies to nestle, sleep and dream. Additionally, **foxgloves, bluebells, and lily-of-the-valley** are the bells fairies ring to announce the start of all their festivities.

Primroses are necessary to render fairies invisible to mortals, **four-o'clocks** (*Mirabilis jalapa*) opening late in the day are fairy time-pieces, and during summer's hot spells, **fairy fans** (*Clarkia breweri*) cool their brows.

Violets, considered a sacred flower and the symbol of fidelity, remembrance, modesty and simplicity are held in great esteem and are used to honor the Fairy Queen on one of the most important of all fairy spring celebrations – the Sacred Violet Festival.

Milkweed (*Asclepias*) pods are used as darling fairy cradles, walnut shells are used to serve food or, for fairy toddlers, as little boats for drifting merrily across a puddle. **Acorn shells** serve as fairy bowls, and **poppy seed pods** (*Papaver*) are perfect for a soothing sip of tea.

Plant **lamb's ear** (*Stachys lanata*) for use as a soft blanket, Queen Anne's lace (*Daucus carota*) for lacy curtains, and **thistle** or **milkweed** (*Asclepias*) provides a soft, downy filling for pillows and covers.

The **fairy slipper** (*Calypso bulbosa*) is an orchid whose blossoms provide fairies with slippers.

For light fairy housekeeping, nothing beats the showy clusters made from the blossoms of the **fairy duster** (*Calliandra eriophylla*).

54

Top, a cozy corner under a jade "tree" where fairies can sit and enjoy this sunny little vegetable garden. Photo courtesy of Miniature Garden Shoppe. Just above, a miniature garden in a small wheelbarrow can be moved around on the whim of the gardener. Photo courtesy of Landscapes in Miniature.

Fairy lanterns (*Calochortus* cvs., especially *C. albus*), nodding blossoms hanging down from graceful stems are carried by fairies to light the way at night.

Chinese lantern plant (*Physalis alkekengi*), with their orange-red, paper-like husks resembling Chinese lanterns, are used by fairies as floor lamps.

The **fairy wand** (*Dierama pendulum*) is a useful scepter for fairy spells, while apple blossoms can be used by the fairies as a portal into a mortal's garden.

For a touch of music, **lily-of-the-valley** (*Convallaria majalis*), **harebell** (*Campanula rotundifolia*) and **coral bells** (*Heuchera* species) chime ever so sweetly as the fairies dance.

And finally, **snapdragons** (*Antirrhinum majus*) are the fierce dragons that not only protect fairies, but provide their transport. Pinching their tiny blossoms makes the dragons roar.

FLOWERS AND PLANTS ASSOCIATED WITH FAIRIES

If there's one thing all gardeners can agree on, it's that fairies love flowers. For believers, fairies bring magic to their gardens, rewarding them with their blessings, which could include good fortune, love, joy and happiness. For non-believers, the magic of fairy gardens is the blessing of a fun project, of creativity and artistry, and of the joy and merriment in the illusion of an imaginary world.

For centuries, numerous cultures made note of which plants were enticing to fairies and which plants offered vulnerable mortals protection from them. Passed down through the generations, it taught peasants the practical considerations of earthly life.

In terms of charms, flowers were at the top of the list, bringing good luck or adversity depending on their use. Though the folklore is a bit ambiguous, the following flowers are believed to be imbued with magical properties. They may be good for warding off fairies or curing the diseases they were believed to cause, or may be the appealing plants which were special or sacred to the fairies.

What fairy wouldn't want to move into this sturdy, thatched-roofed house sitting snugly against a cushiony green sedum lawn. Photo courtesy of Wholesale Fairy Gardens.

So, in the following pages are just a few of the flowers and plants that are associated with fairies and without a doubt can make delightful additions to the landscape. With a bit of research, you may discover more, but this list should give you a great start.

Foxglove (*Digitalis* species). Foxglove is a must-have for attracting fairies to your garden! Fairies play and sleep within the flowers, and each spot or dot inside the blossom is just the mark of a fairy's gentle touch.

Planting foxgloves in the garden is an invitation for fairies to enter. Planted near the front door they are an invitation to your home. Planting them near the home keeps evil at bay, while plucking a stem and bringing it indoors will anger the fairies and bring bad luck. (The name foxglove was derived, ancient legends tell us, when an evil fairy gave a fox the blossoms to put on his toes so that he could rob chicken houses without being heard; hence the name.)

In the unlikely event that your baby is stolen by the fairies, legends say that the juice of foxgloves will help you get it back but do not say how this works.

Primrose (*Primula vulgaris*). Another important plant in the fairy realm, primroses are believed to give fairies their power of invisibility. Hanging a spray of primroses on your door invites the fairy folk to visit and grant their blessings, but scattering primrose blossoms across the threshold creates a barrier against them. Eating primroses lets you see fairies, clutching a bouquet of them could make you invisible, and, conversely, makes the invisible visible. Touching a fairy stone with a posy with the correct number of blossoms opens the door to the world of fairies and fairy gifts, but the wrong number of blossoms in the bouquet brings death. And never, ever grow them indoors as this upsets the fairies and brings about sickness and sorrow.

Thyme (*Thymus*). Plant thyme in your garden and fairies will take up residence, building homes under the mounds. Moonlight thyme (*Thymus leucotrichus*) is probably the most important plant for a fairy garden for legend tells us that fairies hide their babies in the leaves. To invite fairies into your home, sprinkle sprigs of thyme across the threshold and on windowsills or hang in windows. For humans to see fairies a brew must be made from the tops of wild thyme gathered near the side of a fairy hill.

Cowslips (*Primula officinalis*). Loved and protected by fairies, cowslips are helpful to mortals in finding fairy gold. However, fairy gold was notoriously unreliable, appearing as gold when paid, but soon thereafter turning into a variety of useless things.

English Bluebells (*Hyacinthoides nonscripta*). Endemic to Western Europe and especially England, English bluebells are one of the most powerful of all fairy flowers. To call fairies to their midnight dances, the delicate little flowers of bluebells would be rung. However, humans were not allowed to attend these dances, the secrecy of which were so closely guarded that humans who accidentally heard the bells were in mortal danger of dying, hence earning bluebells the added names of warning bells and dead man's bells.

A field of bluebells was especially dangerous as it was considered a place of consecrated fairy magic and enchantment, and people venturing into the woods to pick the flowers would end up wandering endlessly until someone found them and lead them back home.

Top, a petite frog cools in the birdbath surrounded by petite English daisies (*Bellis perennis*). Photo courtesy of Landscapes in Miniature. Just above, rustic steps made of log slices lead to a rustic fairy retreat. Photo courtesy of Jeremie Corp.

Betty Mackey

Betty Mackey

The opening of morning glory blossoms, top, is said to repel unwanted night fairies. Perhaps fairies would make love potions out of these viola petals.

On Beltane (May first) an ankle bracelet made of bluebells and other dangly blossoms attracts helpful sprites.

Ragwort (*Jacobaea vulgaris* syn. *Senecio jacobaea*). Known in Ireland as Fairies' Horse, ragwort was used by fairies as makeshift horses. They would ride to their scenes of midnight merrymaking mounted on the stems of the plant.

Daisy (*Leucanthemum* species). Relaxing in a daisy field helps people connect and make contact with fairies. To keep children safe, place a daisy chain on a child for it is said that a daisy chain will prevent fairies from beguiling the child and carrying him away.

Forget-me-not (*Myosotis* species). The beautiful blue blossoms of forget-me-nots unlock the secrets of the fairies and offer protection from them, too. If you place forget-me-nots on the side of the mountain where fairy treasure is hidden, all doors leading to the secret caverns will open up for you.

Elderberry (*Sambucus* species). Blossoms of the elderberry shrub were used to make fairy wine. When a mortal drinks a home-made brew of elderberry wine he will see a fairy; but if the human drinks elderberry wine from the same goblet as the fairy, he will then be able to see them forever.

Gardenia (*Gardenia* species). Gardenias invoke the protection of children by the fairies, and for those with any telepathic abilities, gardenias will help to increase their abilities.

Harebell (*Campanula rotundifolia*). In folklore, the flowers assist mortals in seeing fairies. When worn as a necklace or wreath the person is incapable of lying. However, some legends tell that the flowers were regarded by some people as unlucky because they could attract evil spirits.

Clover (*Trifolium* species). Clover is considered to be a sacred fairy plant. Clovers of all kinds attract fairies, but the four-leaf clover is noted as being particularly magical. Wearing a four-leaf clover under one's hat while gardening, should enable you to see fairies, if they are present. At the same time, if you anger a fairy, and it tries to cast a spell, the four-leaf clover will break the spell. And as difficult to accomplish as this sounds, it was believed that if you placed seven grains of poppy seed on a four-leaf clover located on your lapel, it would grant the wearer the power to see fairies.

Marigold (*Tagetes* species). It is believed that a wash made from the early morning dew on marigold's petals rubbed around the eyes can give mortals the ability to see fairies.

Morning Glory (*Ipomoea* species). The opening of morning glory blossoms is said to repel unwanted night Fairies.

Pansy (*Viola* species and cultivars). Legend has it that pansies were created by the fairies from the red of sunset, the yellow of sunbeams, the

57

brown of the earth, and the blue of the sky. Petals of these colorful blossoms are used to make strong love potions.

Rose (*Rosa* species and cultivars). Roses, whose sweet scent lures fairies to a garden, also hold the secrets of time. Mere mortals can make fairy love spells by sprinkling rose petals under their feet and dancing softly upon them while at the same time asking the fairies to bestow a blessing on the spell.

Peony (*Paeonia* species). To dream of fairies, place a vase of peony blossoms by your bed. A garland made from peony seeds was once used to protect children from being kidnapped by the fairies.

Violet (*Viola odorata*). Violets are sacred to all fairies because a violet laden glen is the home of the Fairy Queen. Picking the first violet of spring brings mortals good luck and the chance to ask the fairies to grant them a wish.

Lily of the Valley (*Convallaria majalis*). Fairies use lily-of-the-valley blossoms for baby's bonnets and children's hats as well as for making music by ringing the bells.

Carnation (*Dianthus* species). Red carnations are said to attract fairies that heal animals.

Pot Marigold (*Calendula* species). Eating pot marigolds helps mortals to see fairies.

Heather (*Calluna vulgaris*). To ignite a fairy's passion and open the portal between their realm and our world, grow heather. To attract benevolent fairies to your garden, offer a bouquet of heather on the eve of Beltane (May first).

Lady's Mantle (*Alchemilla mollis*). Fairies shower under the dew that drips from the plant's leaves early in the morning.

Lavender (*Lavandula* species). Party lovers that they are, fairies nonetheless favor lavender infused wine as it promotes knowledge. Planting lavender in your garden brings the healing protection afforded by the fairies.

Pearlwort (*Sagina* species). A sprig of the minuscule blossoms hung above the front door is said to prevent fairies from kidnapping any member of the household.

Lilac (*Syringa* species). The sweet scent of lilacs is said to attract fairies to your garden.

Rosemary (*Rosmarinus officinalis*). To keep malicious fairies at bay, scatter sprigs of the herb throughout the house and garden; however, to invite benevolent fairies into your home, burn stems of rosemary as incense.

St. John's Wort (*Hypericum perforatum*). Fairies have been thought to causes all sorts of annoying maladies, from sneezes to itches to cramps. St. John's wort is the chief protective herb against such afflictions. Other herbs in this impressive holy grail of seven fairy herbs are vervain (*Verbena officinalis*), eyebright (*Euphrasia officinalis*), yarrow (*Achillea millefolium*), self-heal (*Prunella vulgaris*), speedwell (*Veronica officinalis*) and mallow (*malva sylvestris*).

Milkweed (*Asclepias* species). If planted in the garden, milkweed will serve as a guarantee that fairies will always be present. Including some of the silky tassels in your pillow helps mortals dream of fairies. In the fall, when the pods burst open and the fluffy seeds fly, a wish is granted for each seed that is caught then released again.

Ferns (small). Although they are not flowers, ferns are a favorite secret hiding place of fairies. There is a tale of a woman who accidentally sat on a fern and as punishment was made to forever reside with fairies,

Betty Mackey

Hypericum is one of seven main fairy herbs and protects users from various minor afflictions.

tending their young. Ferns growing in your landscape are an incentive for fairies to visit.

Oak (*Quercus*), Ash (*Fraxinus*) and **Hawthorn (*Crataegus*)**. These species make up the fairy triad of trees. Where they grow together, legends tell us, fairies live.

Mushrooms and Fairy Rings

In various myths and legends, mushrooms and fairies are strongly associated. Humankind has long been fascinated by the fairy ring, or pixie circle, a natural phenomenon that legends say is created by fairies dancing in a circle on moonlit nights, wearing down the grass beneath their feet. Toads would then sit on the worn-down space, poisoning it and allowing mushrooms to grow, hence the name, toadstool.

The truth is much less romantic, but perhaps needs to be explained. The fact is that a fairy ring is a naturally occurring circle or oval of mushrooms, popping up most often in fields, lawns or forests year after year.

Scientific minds have determined that fairy rings are simply the result of a particular pattern of underground fungi growth that produces the reproductive fruit bodies above ground that we call mushrooms. Because there is no new food for the fungi inside the circle, the process results in

an ever-growing, outwardly expanding, circular direction. That is the scientific explanation at its simplest, devoid of any otherworldly tales.

However, though a little less enchanting, here are a couple of interesting and mysterious facts concerning fairy rings:

■ The rings continue to grow over time. One of the most impressive rings ever found is in France, and though difficult to determine its actual age, the fairy ring is suspected to be about 2,000 feet wide and over 700 years old.

■ Sometimes time, animal droppings, or environmental factors can replenish the missing nutrients inside the ring, resulting in the somewhat rare phenomena of a second ring growing within the first

■ Unlike humans, most grazing animals seem to avoid fairy rings.

Kappi Veenendaal

Mushrooms are important in fairy lore and legends. These are being nourished by a rotting log in the forest.

Fairy Ring Folklore and Superstition. Although we may know the scientific explanation of these fairy rings, they have long been associated with enchanting ideas which have a long history in European folklore. Different cultures view the rings in a similar fashion, but with individual cultural twists.

In Medieval times, circle dancing, or dancing in a circular formation, was the norm at social gatherings. However, with time, English dances became so complex that dancing in a circle or ring was considered not only old-fashioned and foolish but also became associated with fairies or witches.

Thus, when mushroom rings popped up in forests or meadows, they were said to mark the places where fairies had laughed and danced by the light of the moon, wearing down the grass beneath their feet. As fun as that may sound, most cultures viewed them as dangerous places for mortals.

Folklore had it that the lure of fairy music and laughter is known to draw in passersby, and should they be so foolish as to join in the merriment of the dance by stepping into one of these rings, they would be strangely compelled to join the fairies in their wild dancing. Although it felt like the unlucky, exhausted soul had been dancing for minutes, incomprehensibly, they would have been dancing for years. Attempting to rescue a friend, relative, or neighbor was incredibly difficult. The only way these unfortunate captives could be rescued was by having someone outside the ring grab hold of the victim's coat-tails and yank them out.

Enigmatic myths tell us that fairy rings are gateways to the fairy realm, hidden doorways transporting people to other places, other times and dimensions, or into elfin kingdoms where elves gather and forever dance. Other myths tell us that mortals who stepped into an empty fairy ring ended up dying young; those violating fairy perimeters became invisible to people outside the ring; and still others say that fairies force negligent intruders to dance untill they fall exhausted and die, or are forever caught in the throes of madness.

Victorian society believed that fairies were malevolent toward mankind. Scandinavian and Celtic traditions concurred that fairy rings were caused by fairies dancing, warning people against disrupting or joining

Betty Earl

Betty Earl

Top, sitting atop her favorite mushroom, this fairy brings a touch of magic to the outdoor space. Bottom, a charming fairy creates a great sense of motion crossing the bridge within a small window box.

Betty Earl

This ceramic statuette of Zinnia, one of Cicely Mary Barker's Flower Fairies from the *A Flower Fairy Alphabet* series of books, is a charming addition to any garden where she would continue to delight visitors for years to come.

the dance, lest they be punished; Scottish lore has it that the mushrooms are used as resting spots by weary fairies as they dance the night away within the ring, and the Dutch went one step further and attributed the emptiness of the fairy ring to the devil churning his milk.

Austrian superstitions noted that the fairy rings were caused by flying dragons scorching the earth, and once created, nothing but toadstools could ever grow there. The French believed that the rings were guarded by giant bug-eyed toads who cursed all transgressors, and elsewhere in Europe, myths gave rise to the idea that entering a ring could cost the intruder an eye.

But the folklore and superstitions about these fairy rings is not restricted to Europe. Stories of tiny, human-like spirits inhabiting these rings come from the Philippines as well.

According to some traditions, a safe way of investigating a fairy ring is to run counter-clockwise around the ring nine times under the benefit of a full moon, or to wear a hat backwards which would confuse the fairies and prevent them from administering any harm to the wearer.

Despite all the associations of ill luck and doom with the rings, some legends paint fairy rings as places of fertility and fortune or omens of good luck, and even of tales as diverse as granting wishes to improving your looks. Nevertheless, these fairy blessings are not without their maledictions, and tales tell of the sprites finally exacting their revenge.

Today, some gardeners think fairy rings and toadstools are attractive extensions of their yards, while others think of them as weeds. Regardless, I find the rings mysterious and romantic—and definitely nothing to get excited about should one crop up in my garden.

So, when planning a fairy garden, if space permits, I like to curry favor with the fairies by making my own diminutive fairy ring, not by growing real mushrooms, of course, but rather by "growing" a ring of handmade or store bought tiny toadstools.

CICELY MARY BARKER'S FLOWER FAIRIES

Since primeval times, fairies have existed in the beliefs of many cultures. Although each culture had their own interpretation of how fairies looked and what their temperament was, fairies were always considered magical, winged creatures with one tiny foot in their otherworldly realm and the other in our earthly world.

For one of the best ways to learn about the legendary interactions between fairies and plants, turn to British illustrator Cicely Mary Barker's (1895-1973) *Flower Fairies* books and artwork. See the website, www.flowerfairies.com.

For decades, gardeners and non-gardeners alike have been enchanted by Barker's work. The artwork, characterized by the grace and delicacy of her line and colors, depicts a vast and diverse cast of fairies living in our world of meticulously accurate species of flowers, fungi, ferns, and herbs.

The flower fairies look something like beautiful human children, though with pointy ears, captivating eyes and diaphanous wings like those of a butterfly. Other legends and stories tell us that fairies come in all shapes and sizes, but the Flower Fairies are among the smallest.

Over the course of her career, Cicely Mary Barker conceived over 150 individual Flower Fairies and poems, each a brilliantly composed illustration combining fantasy with plant lore, evocatively seducing the reader into a gentle and placidly mysterious realm, where ethereal Flower Fairies busily work and play amid colorful flowers, grassy meadows and on the edge of distant marshes.

Barker's artistic talent and her love of nature enabled her to create an extraordinary world for the Flower Fairies. Though Barker was schooled at home, the flowers and plants contained within were drawn carefully with the precise accuracy of a seasoned botanist. The exquisite watercolors and expressive poems were not only captivating to look at, but impressively informative as well.

Her first book, *Flower Fairies of Spring*, came out in 1923, following the release of *The Coming of the Fairies* by Sir Arthur Conan Doyle, *Peter Pan* by J. M. Barrie and the various fairy-themed works of Ida R. Outhwaite. At this time, people were fascinated with fairies, and *The Flower Fairies of Spring* became an instant hit.

Named after the flower or plant they are destined to forever care for, Flower Fairies were presented as very shy creatures, especially wary of humans.

Simply put, wherever a seed sprouts, a Flower Fairy baby is born. From then on, each Flower Fairy lives and sleeps in his or her designated flower, and as it grows the fairy does too. Presented as a distinctive personality derived from the assigned plant, this identity defines the Flower Fairy's individual aesthetics, disposition, and character. The evocative song each Flower Fairy sings helps guide the spirit of the flower, most of which are commonly found in our gardens.

Flower Fairies are said to be gentle and generous, and exist wherever nature flourished. Passionate in their pursuits, they admired love and beauty and abhorred ugliness and greed.

Superstitions noted that if humans would leave some food or milk for the fairies to dine on and a vessel of clear water for them to bathe in, they would be rewarded with good fortune and the protection of the fairies.

It is said that these Flower Fairies hold certain values in high esteem when dealing with other fairies and these features comprise the Fairy Code: always to be cheerful, neat, polite, friendly, hard working, generous, honest, kind, trustworthy, and humorous.

Today, the Flower Fairies have come a long way from their traditional dwellings. Some believe they only exist in fantasy tales and the imaginations of children but others purchase miniature Flower Fairy statues to add to their fairy gardens as an enticement for real fairies to visit.

Betty Earl

This wee fairy in the smallest of gardens blows happy thoughts to the gardener.

CHAPTER 6: PLANTING, CARE, AND MAINTENANCE OF FAIRY GARDENS

"Of all the minor creatures of mythology, fairies are the most beautiful, the most numerous, the most memorable." ~~~~ Andrew Lang

Fairy gardens can be planted outdoors for year round enjoyment, but you can also enjoy fairy gardens in containers both indoors and out. The planting and care of a fairy garden varies with the type of garden and its growing conditions as well as the placement, environment, and care of the containers you have used.

CREATING OUTDOOR FAIRY GARDENS

You have already chosen the location for your outdoor fairy garden, and based on the microclimate and exposure have picked the plants that will be happy in the amount of light and the soil type that you have, as well as in your USDA hardiness zone. Plants are living things that cannot adjust to all conditions, but will thrive when you select the right plants for your environment and give them the care they need.

In general, trying to grow outdoor plants indoors will not work. Watering plants too often that like to be kept on the dry side will not work, and allowing plants that enjoy wet feet to experience drought will not work, either. Visit your local nursery or garden center for advice. Employees care about plants and know what works in your area and climate zone.

Hopefully, you have laid out a design on paper as this will make it easier to proceed. But if not, don't fret. Though the procedure might be more of a trial and error process, it will still be fun.

Early prep work. Before planting, prepare your soil by pulling out all weeds and grass roots, then work in soil amendments like compost to ensure the success of your plants. Choose a day that is on the cooler, cloudier side as the conditions on a hot, sunny day are quite stressful for plants. If you haven't had rain or watered the area for close to a week, give it a good watering a day or two beforehand. If your plants are dry in their pots, water them first to get them moist before planting.

Placement of structures. Start by placing your fairy house in its desired location. Then lay out the major components: such as paths, sparkling rivers, streams, and ponds, a sitting area or dining space, bridges, patios, arbors and gazebos as well as fencing or walls by drawing lines in the dirt—or if you are comfortable with it, in your head—allocating space to each designation. There could already be some plants in the space you've chosen for the in-ground fairy garden, so either work around them, or dig them up for reloca-

Encircling a miniature tree, the under-the-tree garden seat provides fairies with a shady place to relax and enjoy a frosted glass of iced tea.

Betty Earl

63

tion. Keep it simple, as too many elements in your design can give the fairy garden a cluttered look.

Plants. You've already chosen the plants—low-growing herbs, groundcovers and perennials—keeping in mind your site conditions and requirements. The scale of the plants in relation to your fairy house is an important aspect, as the plants create the miniature landscape of your fairy garden. Study the information on the plant tags in deciding how far apart to plant.

Place the purchased plants still in their pots approximately where you would like to plant them in your fairy garden, locating taller, larger plants toward the back of the garden and the shorter ones towards the front. View the design from all angles making adjustments as necessary, spacing the plants far enough apart to allow for mature growth in years to come.

How to plant. Dig holes that are wider but not deeper than the container, big enough to accommodate the plant's root systems. Working with one plant at a time, remove the plant from its container by tapping the sides of the container or gently squeezing the pot to loosen the plant, and turning plant and container upside down so that the plant easily slides out into your hand. Inspect the roots, if they are circling, gently tease them apart. If the plant is root bound and impossible to tease apart by hand, make four shallow cuts into the root mass near the bottom with a sharp knife, promoting new growth into the soil.

Now, carefully place the plant roots in the hole and cover with soil, making sure the plant is planted at the same depth as it was in the container. Never try to shoehorn a plant into a hole that's too small for it. Fill in with soil, gently pressing the soil into place with your fingers and water thoroughly. If needed, add more soil to fill indentations when the dirt settles.

Do not fertilize at this point. Wait a week or so to allow roots to grow in a bit before fertilizing with a water-soluble fertilizer.

Keep a watchful eye on newly planted perennials, watering them whenever the top two to three inches of soil dry out, but don't kill them with kindness. Understand that some plants may struggle and die or outgrow your intended design or that you might need to fill in some areas with annuals until the perennials mature.

Hardscaping and Accessories. If you've planted many plants and the entire future in-ground fairy garden area is quite wet, wait a day for the soil to dry a bit before proceeding with the hardscaping. It will be less muddy and easier to work with.

Now place decorative accessories within the garden area to promote the fairy theme. As in your own backyard landscaping, tackle the biggest jobs first. Build a pathway made of flat stones, tiles or pebbles for the fairies to walk on or a large flat stone to hold a decorative café table and chairs. Locate arbors, gazebos or trellises in their designated places. Add a pond or a stream and a bridge because fairies love the sound and sight of water. Add miniature chairs or benches for seating and partying, then finish the design by incorporating small accessories such as wheelbarrows, gazing balls, bird baths, and mini-potted plants. Add a fairy statue or two to entice the wee folk to visit.

Remember that fine-tuning your outdoor fairy garden is a process that can take days or even weeks to complete. Don't rush it. You may find new accessories that appeal to your imagination, or a different location for the old ones. Tap into your imagination and enjoy the journey.

This fountain with running water enhances fairy gardens.

Betty Earl

Instructions for Container Fairy Gardens

As mentioned, any bowl or container that has a good-sized open area that can hold soil and also allow water to properly drain is a good choice. If the container is a wicker basket or other "holey" pot that will be located indoors, line it with plastic—a similar sized plastic bag works best, cut to fit with edges rolled back inside the container about an inch below the rim. If the very porous container will be kept outside, line it with burlap for proper drainage, again, cut back to about an inch below the rim.

Before buying them you should decide whether the plants you select will be moisture loving or desert-type plants. You cannot mix the two in a single container because attention to the right amount of watering is a must. Keep the old saying "right plant, right place" uppermost in your mind. Group the plants with the same water and light requirements together in the same container. There is no compromising on this matter. Any plant that is not in the right spot will succumb to a slow death.

Use a high quality sterilized, commercially available potting mix for the soil. Most quality blends consist of approximately three equal amounts of compost, peat or coir, and pumice, vermiculite or perlite. Avoid potting mixes that contain added fertilizers or wetting agents, and always follow specific care recommendations about watering for your plant choices.

Potting mixtures are available in different sized bags, allowing you to purchase only the amount you need at the time. Do not use garden dirt or mixes containing dirt, as they will not drain properly. Unlike dirt, a sterilized potting mix contains no weed seeds or soil-borne diseases.

If your fairy garden consists of succulent plants, purchase a potting mix designated for such use. Most succulent plants, including cacti, need a fast-draining soil mix containing horticultural grade sand and grit.

Points to consider before you plant. If your outdoor container fairy garden will be permanently located under an overhang or enclosure, containers with drain-age holes or without can both be considered. However, if your outdoor container fairy garden will be exposed to the elements, you MUST use a container with adequate drainage holes. Otherwise, water will collect in your pot leading to root rot and the plants will die.

No one wants to see their cherished plants die, but it happens sometimes, so don't beat yourself up if it does. Remember, some plants, like people, are very easy-going and put up with most kinds of treatment, while others are prima-donnas requiring you to wait on them hand-and-foot. So choose the right plant for the right environment. For your indoor container fairy gardens, the key to success is simple: learn where your plants originated and provide these same basic conditions as best you can. Keep the following six main reasons for the demise of plants uppermost in your mind, and you'll find you and your plants can live happily together.

1) Over watering. Probably the number one killer of foliage plants in containers is over watering. Plants in overly wet conditions tend to wilt, prompting the owner to apply even more water, making a bad situation worse. Soil dries from the top down, so just because the top feels dry, doesn't mean it is time to add more water. Feel the potting mix and inch or two down or heft the container in deciding when to water. With practice, you will get the hang of it.

Even fairies enjoy growing various types of vegetables as seen in this neat and tidy garden complete with bee skeps. Photo courtesy of Jeremie Corp.

At the bend of a mulched pathway located under a dense canopy of deciduous trees and conifers, visitors to the garden happily stumble upon this woodsy fairy house. The fairy door, located at ground level, leads fairies up a hidden staircase to the house situated on an old tree stump which gives fairies a great view of the garden—and if frightened a beautiful house to hide in.

2) Drought or Neglect. The flip side of over watering is neglect. If plants become overly dry, do not pour excessive amounts of water, nor let the containers sit in standing water for periods of time. Just wet them back to reasonable levels and try to establish a regular watering schedule.

3) Fertilization. Plants growing in low-light interior environments need a lot less fertilization than plants growing in bright-light, full sun conditions. Contain the urge to fertilize regularly.

4) Low Light. Foliage plants are generally quite tolerant of low light conditions; however, keep in mind that growers generally produce these plants under much brighter light levels to increase growth rates. Acclimate plants to your environment by first keeping them in brighter light before transitioning them to their permanent location.

5) Temperature and Humidity. Tropical plants find cold drafts or cold weather particularly troublesome, so make sure to keep them at temps no lower than 60° F and out of direct drafts from air conditioners. Low humidity brought about by heating can also be damaging to plants. Keeping them on trays of pebbles and water, or adding a humidifier to a room, will work wonders.

6) Pests. You need to be vigilant here. Small problems are easily contained, but once populations of insects and mites become large, they are hard to control. The same dry, hot air that plants resent is very favorable for mite, scale and mealy bug infestations. Adopt a watchful attitude, checking the undersides of leaves for potential problems.

Planting your indoor and outdoor containers. If your container has drainage holes, cover the holes with coffee filters to keep the potting mix from washing out. It is advisable to place a watertight tray under the container to catch excess water as well as to protect the table or any other surface from water damage.

The next step for containers with and without drainage holes is the addition of about two inches of a drainage layer consisting of pea gravel, crushed rock, pebbles, feather rock, or broken pieces of clay or terra cotta pots. This layer is important since it collects excess moisture away from the potting mix, keeps the plant roots from sitting in soggy soil, and gives roots access to oxygen. (Hint: to prevent potential insect and disease problems, I wash my gravel, pebbles, etc. in hot water before adding to the container.) At this point, I prefer to cover the drainage layer with a piece of hardware cloth, window screening, coffee filters, or even a piece of nylon stocking to keep charcoal and soil from sifting down into this layer.

Now, add a thin layer (a half inch is more than enough) of activated charcoal. You can also add the charcoal to the potting mix. The purpose of the charcoal is to keep the potting mix "sweet." Finally, add a high quality sterilized, commercial potting mix, the soil level to within ¾ to 1 inch of the rim of the planter. You should have at least three inches of potting mix, enough to adequately support the plant root system.

Left, a layer of pebbles is added for drainage, then coffee filters or screening are overlaid to keeps most of the charcoal and soil from washing down into the pebbles. Top, then horticultural charcoal is added to keep the soil sweet. Center, if plants need dividing, gently pull the root mass apart, and (bottom) pot each plant at the same depth it was growing in the container. Photos by Betty Earl.

Here is the newly planted fairy garden in the container.

Generally, you will not have to fertilize container fairy gardens because rapid growth is not desirable for plants inside them. Plus, the plants will seldom be in there long enough to deplete nutrients from the soil, before they are divided and repotted or moved to larger containers. That said, if the plants have been in place for a long time and start to show signs of weakness or nutrient deficiency, feed them with a very dilute strength house plant food.

Plants selected for indoor fairy gardens which need higher humidity should be misted occasionally to achieve lush foliage. Whether grown indoors or out, plants in containers are best watered with non-softened water as most are sensitive to chemicals. If you do not have access to non-softened water, allow your tap water to set for 24 hours so that chlorine and other chemicals can dissipate from it. If your landscape design includes variable soil elevations, the gradient changes should be formed with additional potting mix.

Outdoor fairy garden containers need to be protected from strong winds and heavy rains, and generally do better with morning sun and afternoon shade. As with other outdoor container gardens, instructions for over-wintering outdoor fairy gardens vary. Different parts of the country have different winter weather conditions. It is best to con-

sult the local nursery or garden center where you purchased your plants for recommendations.

Once you've prepped the soil, make a test layout of your design, placing plants, furniture and accessories, such as patios, paths, arbors, and benches in their respective proposed places on top of the soil. This is your last opportunity to fine tune your design without making a big mess. Make whatever adjustments are necessary. Then remove these items and begin planting.

Start with the plants that have the largest root mass or the tallest plants. Scoop out a hole where the plant is to be located, remove the plant from the nursery container, put the plant in the hole, and smooth out the soil. Repeat this procedure with the remaining plants. Each plant should be set into the garden at the same depth it was growing in the pot, neither too shallowly nor too deep.

Should some plants need to be divided before planting, remove them from their containers and gently pull the root mass apart using your fingers.

Once the fairy garden planting is finished, give the garden an initial watering with tepid water using a small watering can with fine holes, delivering a gentle spray of water, completely soaking the potting mix. Cold water may shock the plants, and as mentioned softened water should never be used

Damp (not wet) soil will make it easier to lay or move the pebbles, tiles, or gravel on the soil as needed for pathways, patios, or streams and will keep them from mixing with the soil and looking messy.

Add garden ornamentation such as arbors, bridges, and tools. If an accessory is very light and small, top heavy, or hard to keep upright, consider attaching a small screw or wire to its base to act as an underground stake.

Watering container fairy gardens is best done by hand, using a watering can with a fine spray. Too much water poured out too fast can leave holes and scatter small accessories, ruining the design.

Watering schedules change throughout the year. Plants in active growth in spring and summer require more water than they do during the winter months. For the succulent or dry dish fairy garden, allow the soil to

Set on sand, a raised area defined by pebbles is the perfect spot for a bench for fairies to sit and enjoy the sunny little indoor garden or sip some cool lemonade at the cafe table and chairs. Photo courtesy of Jeremie Corp.

Betty Earl

Fairy gardens are for everyone! Above, people with allergies to plants or those with "brown thumbs" can still enjoy a fairy garden composed in a Victorian-style terrarium, complete with a place for fairies to relax and enjoy a cup of tea. Top right, a wizard hides near the fairy house, and (bottom, right) tiny clay "gourds" awaiting the arrival of Purple Martins. Photos, top right, courtesy of Longwood Gardens; bottom right, courtesy of Jeremie Corp.

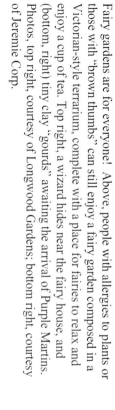

"GARDEN FAIRIES COME AT DAWN,
BLESS THE FLOWERS THEN
THEY'RE GONE"

~~~~~ AUTHOR UNKNOWN

dry almost completely between waterings to prevent root rot. Succulents will require a more frequent watering schedule in the spring and summer and less water in late summer and fall. In winter, when plants slow down, keep watering to a minimum.

Your fingertip is one of your best assets when it comes to gauging water needs. For moisture loving plants, keep the soil moist, never soggy. For succulent gardens, if the soil feels moist about an inch down, wait until it dries a bit more before watering.

AND IN CONCLUSION

Without a doubt, fairy gardens are addictive. Just as you are finishing up designing and planting one, your imagination kicks into high gear and you start making plans for the next one. And, unless they are scattered helter-skelter all over the place, that is not a bad thing.

However, before you embark on that next creation, my advice is to slow down and enjoy the one you've just created. Savor the moment. Ask yourself, will you still like it as it is two weeks down the line, or will you find the need to move, delete, or even add plants or accessories to the design. Sometimes it's the smallest of details that can take your design from good to outstanding.

Maybe the addition of a mini tea set on the café table and a few potted mini containers brings some much needed color and pizzazz to a shady area, or a Chip and Dale bridge needs a few more stone steps on either side to make it easier for fairies to get on and off the bridge. Possibly you find that the plantings could use more or fewer blossoms, so you change or replace a few plants. Give yourself the time and opportunity to find that out.

That said, if you find yourself inclined to add more fairy houses and gardens in-ground outdoors, in containers scattered about your patio or deck, or even indoors, displayed on shelves, counters or table tops, find a way to tie them together. It is important. Don't let your collection lose cohesiveness. Resist the temp-

tation to add so many sweet accessories that your design becomes chaotic. Favor order and tidiness.

If your yard is small, think of your multiple fairy gardens as a friendly urban "fairy-hood." See them as small little plots within your garden with fairy houses and gardens separated by mini hedges or mini fences with individual landscaping both in front and back of these little houses. As in any urban environment, the houses and landscaping around them need not be the same, but they should not be jarring or unacceptable to the wee neighbors, even if the neighbors are fairies.

If your garden is large, when adding multiple houses, think in terms of "fairy suburbia." Houses can be set a bit farther apart, at angles to one another, with pathways connected to a common passageway. Some fairy lots might have streams or ponds, others might sport picket fences surrounding veggie gardens out back, others might overflow with floriferous beds and borders, yet all are complemented with a wide variety of "trees," "shrubs" and flowers. But most important of all, this fairy suburbia should fit aesthetically within your landscaping.

If your fairy gardens are in containers out in the garden or on a deck or patio, you have more flexibility because you can move them around with the seasons or as the mood strikes you. Indoor container fairy gardens or tablescapes can be designed to fit the decor of the room, or if they are primarily foliage, can be easily grouped together or spread out over several locations.

Spend a little quality time with each miniature fairy garden getting into the rhythm of its cultural care before moving on to the next one. Above all, give flight to your imagination and have fun. Let that inner child inside you —or those close to you— soar.

Betty Earl

71

FURTHER READING

Barker, Cicely Mary, The Flower Fairies series. Now published in Warne, Germany and by Penguin USA. See also www.flowerfairies.com. Titles include:

Fairyopolis: A Flower Fairies Journal
Hidden Flower Fairies,
How to Find Flower Fairies
The Girls' Book of Flower Fairies
The Complete Book of the Flower Fairies
Flower Fairies Alphabet
Flower Fairies of the Autumn
Flower Fairies of the Garden
Flower Fairies of the Spring
Flower Fairies of the Summer
Flower Fairies of the Trees
Flower Fairies of the Wayside
Flower Fairies of the Winter
Flower Fairies Magical Doors
Return to Fairyopolis

Cross, Tom & Lewis, Constance Barkley, *Fairy Garden: Fairies of the Four Seasons*, Andrews McMeel Publishing, Riverside, NJ, 1998

Heffernan, Maureen, *Fairy Houses of the Maine Coast*, Down East Books, Rockport, ME, 2010

Kane, Tracy, *Fairy Houses...Everywhere!*, (The Fairy House Series), Light-Beams Publishing, Lee, NH, 2006

Kane, Tracy, *Fairy Houses and Beyond!*, (The Fairy House Series), Light-beams Publishing, Lee, NH, 2008

Martin, Laura, and Martin, Cameron, *Fairy Island: An Enchanted Tour of the Homes of the Little Folk*, Black Dog & Leventhal Publishers, New York, NY, 2005

Virtue, Doreen, Ph.D., *Fairies 101: An Introduction to Connecting, Working, and Healing with the Fairies and Other Elementals*, Hay House, Carlsbad, CA and Others, 3rd edition, 2011

RESOURCES

Wholesale. The following vendors are wholesale only and are noted for information about the kinds of things that are available. I suggest checking their web sites for ideas, then checking with your local garden center or nursery to see if they carry or can order the items you find interesting.

Dwarf Conifers

Iseli Nursery
www.iselinursery.com

Fairy Garden Houses and Accessories
Jeremie Corp.
www.jeremiecorp.com

Wholesale Fairy Gardens
www.wholesalefairygardens.com

Online retail sources. The following are online retail vendors for fairy garden houses, doors, and accessories, presented here as stepping stones into the world of fairy gardens. Many local garden centers and nurseries carry a wide assortment of these items, so take the time to check them out. And if none of this catches your fancy, Google for your needs on-line.

Miniature Garden Shoppe
www.miniaturegardenshoppe.com

Enchanted Gardens
www.miniature-gardens.com

The Enchanted World of Fairy Woodland
www.fairywoodland.com

The Fairy's Garden
www.thefairysgarden.com

Market Hill
www.finefairyhouses.com

Wee Trees
www.weetrees.com

INDEX

Finished Gardens

Landscapes in Miniature
www.landscapesinminiature.com

Plants for fairy gardens. For indoor and outdoor fairy garden suitable plants, try your local independent garden center, nursery or big box store. Some stock an incredible diversity of suitable plants. However, if you are looking for something rare or unusual, or if your local venues do not carry plants you are searching for, try searching for plants on the internet. Miniature and rock garden plants often do well.

To get you started, here are a few good **on-line retail plant sources:**

Batson's Foliage Group, Inc. (Ittie Bitties Division)
www.batsononline.com/ittie-bitties-2

Glasshouse Works
www.glasshouseworks.com

Jeepers Creepers®
www.jeeperscreepers.info

Pepper's Greenhouses
(Mail Order Plant Division)
www.accentsforhomeandgarden.com

Stepables®
www.Stepables.com

Simply Succulents®
www.simplysucculents.com

Acaena species, 42
accessories, 8,9, 14,15,17, 20, 23,29,33,34,48,64
Achillea tomentosa, 40
Acoris gramineus, 39
African Violet, 44
Ajuga, 38
Alcea rosea, 54
Alchemilla mollis, 58
Alpine Geranium, 40
Alpine Speedwell, 40
Alternanthera, 47
Anacyclus depressus, 42
Ann Arbor, and fairy doors, 31-33
Anthemis carpatica, 42
Antirrhinum majus, 55
arbors, 34
Arctostaphyllos uva-ursi, 40
Arenaria balearica, 39
Armeria maritima, 41
Asclepias species, 54,58
Baby Tears, 38, 46
Baby's Breath, 42
Barker, Cecily Mary, 50,61-2
Bearberry, 40
Begonia partita, 47
Beltane, 15
Blue Star Creeper, 40
Boxwood, 43, 47
Brass Buttons, 40
bridge, 33, 34
Broom, 43
Bugleweed, 38
Buxus sempervirens, 43, 47
Cacti, 47,65
Calendula species, 58
Calico Plant, 47
Calluna species, 58
Calypso bulbosa, 54
Campanula rotundifolia, 57
Carnation, 58
chairs, 34
changelings, 13
Chiastophyllum oppositifolium, 41
children, and fairy gardens, 5,9,13,18-20, 29

Chinese Lantern, 55
Cinquefoil, 40
Clover, 57
Columbine, 54
Comprosma kirkii, 47
conifers, 43
container fairy gardens, 35,44
  outdoor, 65-71
  container gardens, indoor, 35
Convallaria majalis, 58
Corsican Sandwort, 39
Cotyledon, 41
crafts, and fairy gardens, 27 28,29, 49,50
Crassula argentea, 47
Cuphea hyssopifolia, 43
Cymbalaria muralis, 39
Daisy, 57
Delosperma cooperi, 42
Dianthus, 41, 58
Dierama pendulum, 55
Digitalis species, 54,55
dish gardens, 44. See Containers.
door, fairy, 9,28,29-32
doorknobs, and fairies, 30
drainage, 67
ecology, and fairy lore, 13, 17,18
Elderberry, 57
Eleocharis radicans, 40
elf locks, 52
English Bluebells, 56
environment, and fairy lore, 13,17,18
Episcia dianthiflora, 45
Erigeron trifidus, 42
Erodium reichardii, 40
Faerie. See fairy and fairies.
fairies, 9,13,17,18,27,28,29,50,51
  belief in, 5, 7, 11-15
fairy doors, 9, 29-33
fairy gardens
  accessories for, 48-50
  creation of 7-9,17-2,25-6, 33, 63-70
  furnishings for, 8,9,14,15,17,20,23
  location of, 8,18,19,25, 64
  indoor, 23, 63-70
  outdoor, 19-21,23, 36-43
  planting of, 63-70

73

Betty Earl

Mini succulents in half-inch clay pots. Duane Campbell.

fairy houses, 17, 20, 22, 24-28
Fairy Lanterns, 55
fairy rath, 53
fairy rings, 9, 59-61
Fairy Slipper, 54
Fairy Wand, 55
False Heather, 43
fencing, 33, 35
ferns, 46, 58
fertilizer, 64, 65, 66, 68
Fittonia albivenis, 46
Flag, miniature golden sweet, 39
Fleabane, 43
Flower Fairies books, 61-2
folklore, 7, 11-15, 27, 28, 29, 51, 55
Forget-Me-Not, 57
Foxglove, 54, 55
Gardenia, 57
gazebo, 10, 34
Genista pilosa, 43
Golden Bird's Foot, 42
Gypsophila cerastioides, 42
hardiness, plant, 36-43
hardscaping, 64

Harebell, 57
Heather, 58
Hebe buxifolia, 47
Hedera helix, 46
Hemigraphis 'Exotica', 45
Hemingraphis 'Exotica', 45
herbs, 35, 37, 53, 58. See names.
Herniaria glabra, 41
Hollyhock, 54
Hosta, 39
houses, fairy, 17, 20, 22, 24-28
humidity, indoors, 68
Hyacinthoides nonscripta, 56
Hypericum perforatum, 58
Hypoestes phyllostacha, 45
Ice Plant, 42
Ipomoea species, 57
Irish Moss, 41, 53
Isotoma fluviatilis, 40
Ivy, 46
Jade Plant, 47
Japanese Holly Fern, 47
Kenilworth Ivy, 39
Lace Flower, 45
Lady's Mantle, 58
Lavandula species, 58
Lavender, 58
legends, 52
legends, 7, 11-15, 52
Leptinella squalida, 40
Leucanthemum species, 57
light, 66
lighting, indoor, 44
Lily of the Valley, 58
Linaria lobatus, 40
Lindernia grandiflora, 42
Lithodora, 43
Lobelia chinensis, 42
Lotus corniculatus, 42
Maidenhair vine, 45
maintenance, 63-71
Marigold, 57
Mazus reptans, 39
Milkweed, 54, 58
Mirror Plant, 47
mirrors, 52
Mondo Grass, 40, 45

Moneywort, 42
moon cycle, and fairies, 15
Morning Glory, 57
Mosaic Plant, 46
Mt. Atlas Daisy, 42
Muehlenbeckia complexa, 45
mushrooms, 9, 59-61
Myrtle, 47
Myrtus communis minima, 47
Nasturtium, 54
nature, and fairies, 13, 17-20, 28
Nerve Plant, 46
New Zealand Bur, 42
Ophiopogon japonicus, 40, 45
Oxalis regnellii, 45
Paeonia species, 58
Pansy, 57
paths, 33
Peony, 58
Peperomia, 46
pests, indoors, 66
Picea glauca, 43
Pilea species, 45
Pinks, 41
planting. See also fairy gardens.
   and design, 16, 36-7
   of containers, 67-68
   for fairies, 52-58
   indoor, 44-47
   of outdoor garden, 36-43,
     63-4
plants, 8, 16, 33-58
   and exposure, 36-43
   care of, 63-71
Polka Dot Plant, 45
poppy, 54
Pot Marigold, 58
Potentilla cvrs, 40
Primrose, 56
Primula species, 56
Ragwort, 57
Rhodiola pachyclados, 41
Rose, 58
Rosemary, 52, 58
Ruellia caroliniensis, 43

Rupturewort, 41
Rush, 40
Sagina subulata, 41, 53
Saintpaulia ionantha, 44
Sambucus species, 57
Saxifraga stolonifera, 46
Scotch Moss, 41, 53
Sea Thrift, 41
Sedum species, 42
Selaginella kraussiana, 46
shade, outdoor plants for, 38
Shamrock Plant, 45
Snapdragon, 54
Snowy Marguerite, 55
Soleirolia soleirolii, 38, 46
Speedwell, 39, 40
St. John's Wort, 58
Stonecrop, 41, 42
Strawberry begonia, 46
Succulents, 45, 47, 65
Sweet Peas, 54
Tagetes species, 57
temperature, indoors, 66
theme, 25
Thrift, 41
Thyme, 42, 53, 56
Toadflax, 40
topography, 34
trees, 59
Trifolium species, 57
Tropaeolum majus, 54
Turkish Speedwell, 41
Veronica species, 39, 40, 41
Viola species, 39, 54, 57, 58
Virtue, Doreen, 13
Waffle Plant, 45
water,
   and design, 34
   and fairies, 9, 52
watering, 65-6, 68-9
Wild Petunia, 42
Wire Vine, 45
Wooly Turkish Veronica, 41
Wooly Yarrow, 40
Wright, Jonathan, 31

About the Author

Betty Earl is an author, writer, lecturer, and photographer based in Northern Illinois. Her articles have appeared in *American Nurseryman, Midwest Living Magazine, Small Gardens, Backyard Solutions, Old Farmers Almanac, Nature's Garden, Chicagoland Gardening Magazine,* and elsewhere. She writes regularly for the *Kankakee Daily Journal,* and the *Diggin' It* blog on *The Christian Science Monitor.* The regional representative for the *Garden Conservancy,* she gardens on some of the worst clay/road fill "soil" in the state. Her website is www.BettyEarl.com.

A Note from B. B. Mackey Books

This book and many other fine books about gardening published by B. B. Mackey Books may be found at certain bookstores and botanical gardens, can be gotten by special order from full service bookstores, and can be purchased online from www.amazon.com and from www.mackeybooks.com, among other sources.

Not every fairy garden has to be located in a traditional container. Here, a wee stone house next to a dwarf conifer is surrounded by various sedum in shades of blue/green, enhanced by the blueness of the roof and the gray and slate blue mix of pebbles. Photos courtesy of Landscapes in Miniature.

Lightning Source UK Ltd.
Milton Keynes UK
UKRC02n1609300717
306279UK00002B/34